Look at any horse's head. Is his profile straight, or does he have a Roman nose, a dish face, or a bump below his eyes? Are his eyes large and soft, almond-shaped, or hooded and half-closed? Are his ears broad and set wide apart, or are they fine, fluted, and narrow at the top? What about his mouth, lips, nostrils, muzzle, chin, and jowls? All these different parts of his face — in combination — will give you a clue to his personality. He could be an uncomplicated sort: confident, intelligent, a horse who learns easily. Or he could have a difficult, mercurial personality requiring great patience and understanding on the part of his owner.

Linda Tellington-Jones explains how to analyze the meaning of all these physical traits that indicate the horse's true personality — his inborn character. She then teaches you to determine if the horse's personality has been affected adversely by stress or pain caused by poor health, inadequate living conditions, or a riding discipline not suited to the horse's conformation. Most importantly, she explains how you can develop a deeper understanding in order to bond with your horse and influence his personality in a positive way.

In addition to more than two hundred photographs and drawings, there are pictures of twenty-one horses of various breeds that the author uses to demonstrate her technique of personality analysis. She also gives advice on "matchmaking" (how to find the right horse for you), as well as offering some tips and tools to help you influence his character. These include her revolutionary "touches" and exercises that help calm a horse, restore his confidence, and ease any pain, fear, or tension.

Linda Tellington-Jones is the internationally recognized equine expert who developed the Tellington TTouch. This method of healing, training, and communication can be accomplished by horsemen of all levels. She was honored as 1994 Horsewoman of the Year by the North American Horsemen's Association and presented with the ARICP (American Riding Instructor Certification Program) Lifetime Achievement Award, given annually to a person who profoundly affects the equine world in a positive manner. The author of several books and many videos on horse training, she is also the founder of TTEAM, the Tellington-Jones Equine Awareness Method. She lives in Santa Fe, New Mexico.

Sybil Taylor is the author of several books, as well as the co-author of The Tellington TTouch. *She lives in New York City.*

Getting in TTouch
Understand and Influence Your Horse's Personality

Also by Linda Tellington-Jones

Endurance and Competitive Trail Riding
(with Wentworth Tellington)

The Tellington-Jones Equine Awareness Method
(with Ursula Bruns)

The Tellington TTouch
(with Sybil Taylor)

Getting in TTouch

Understand and Influence Your Horse's Personality

Linda Tellington-Jones

with Sybil Taylor

Trafalgar Square Publishing

NORTH POMFRET, VERMONT

First published in 1995
by Trafalgar Square Publishing
North Pomfret, Vermont 05053

Library of Congress Cataloging-in-Publication Data

Tellington-Jones, Linda.
    Getting in ttouch : understand and
influence your horse's personality / by Linda
Tellington-Jones, with Sybil Taylor.
        p.   cm.
    Includes index.
    ISBN 1-57076-018-7
    1. Horses—Behavior.
    2. Horses—Anatomy.
    3. Horses—Training.
    I. Taylor, Sybil.
    II. Title.
SF281.T44 1995
636.1'083—dc20   94-37475
                                             CIP

ISBN: 1-57076-018-7

Printed in the United States of America

10 9 8 7 6 5 4 3 2 1

Dedication

This book is dedicated to my sister, Robyn Hood, with my deepest appreciation for the major contributions she has made to my life; to the memory of my Grandfather George, who taught me to approach horses with gentleness; to the memory of Grandfather Will Caywood, who gifted me with his understanding of equine nature and gypsy lore; and to the spirit of all the horses who have enriched my life and opened my heart.

Acknowledgments

I offer my collective gratitude to the many hundreds of horse enthusiasts who, over the past 20 years, have taken the time to photograph their horses for personality analysis.

I especially wish to thank my publisher, Caroline Robbins, for her support and encouragement in the writing of this book and for her many hours of patient advice and precise editing. And thanks also to Martha Cook for her painstaking efforts in pulling together all the pieces.

My deepest gratitude to Went Tellington for the hours he spent sitting around the kitchen table with my grandfather, Will Caywood, drawing out his memories of Russia and gypsy lore, and also for teaching me to be a keen observer and to share that information freely with the horse world.

My thanks to Robert Whiteside, who spent precious hours with me in the summer of 1975, encouraging me to hone my observations of equine personality based on head shape.

Photographers Jodi Frediani and Jane Reed worked diligently to find the horses pictured in this book. For their dedication, advice, and endless hours of work—in the field, in the darkroom, and on the phone—I thank them. My appreciation also to Denny Egan for his extensive and skillful work in advising and assisting Jane Reed with the photography.

My gratitude to artists Susan Harris and Jean MacFarland for their excellent drawings, which have added so much to this book, and for their patience in refining the drawings to exact detail.

There are no adequate words to acknowledge the contribution of my sister, Robyn Hood. I thank her for her insistence that kept me writing personality evaluations for *TTeam News International,* for all her suggestions for the third chapter of this book, The Elements of Analysis, and for her observations and assistance over the past two decades.

I also wish to thank Ursula Bruns for encouraging me to develop TTeam work into a system and for her interest in personality analysis.

I am grateful to Professor James Beery, whose drawings of wild-eyed horses so piqued my childhood imagination and thus inspired me to explore the "reading" of equine personality.

For their friendship, interest, and assistance, I wish to acknowledge and thank Lothar, Eve and Amanda Karla, Wolf Krober, Erika Meuller, Kate Riordan, Doris and Kerry Churchill, Elizabeth Furth, Carol Lang, Anne Kursinski, Joyce Harmon, Simona Gallo, Ulla von Kaiser, Michaela Christian and Joyce Anderson.

For years, this book was my dream project. It would not have come to fruition without my co-author, Sybil Taylor, and her patience, skill, and thought-provoking questions. I wish to thank her on behalf of all the horses who will be understood in new ways and for all those who will see their equine partners with new eyes.

Contents

PART TWO

HEALTH: ITS EFFECT ON PERSONALITY

PART THREE

BRING OUT THE BEST IN YOUR HORSE

Foreword

In a horse world steeped in convention, Linda Tellington-Jones is a breath of fresh air. Dynamic, lighthearted and ever inquisitive, her teachings are likewise inventive, playful and far-reaching. Approach Linda and her work, and you are assured of being challenged. Come with an open mind, and you'll be transformed. While modern science and culture have sought to understand and control the world around us through fragmentation and specialization—and our beloved horses have not been immune from this fate—Linda has set out to integrate the parts into a whole anew. Focusing on the parts, we run the risk of thinking of the horse in mechanistic terms; Linda's work re-integrates the fragments, and the unified horse reemerges as a unique being, to be treated with greater respect, patient understanding and outright admiration.

Getting in TTouch is a joy to read on several levels. It is an encyclopedic presentation of every conceivable element and clue that play into the personality mix, from the formal to the traditional. Students of the horse will be permanently enriched by the scope of information contained between these covers. For the more casual reader, the book is a powerful eye opener alerting us to the price we pay for ignorance, no matter how benign. If we fail to see the horse as a whole, Linda clearly illustrates, we are doomed to draw misguided conclusions at the most inauspicious moments. Still more, *Getting in TTouch* offers a lucid exposition of the fundamentals of Linda's innovative and unquestionably effective methods of teaching, healing, and transforming horses and their riders. TTEAM work doesn't just look simple; it is simple and readily accessible to anyone willing to devote a few minutes each day to its potent practice. Finally, Linda's personal style shines through the book. Page after quick page, the anecdotes and case studies of horses she has helped will hold you fascinated as they teach you new ways to deal with horses. You are even likely to adjust your essential beliefs of what is true about horses to accommodate these insights.

I knew a dozen years ago when a three-part series in *EQUUS* introduced Linda to an international audience that she was no ordinary voice. I have even greater admiration for her now, seeing how her work has evolved and grown. That work, I am sure, is by no means completed; it won't be, so long as Linda remains in the presence of horses.

Ami Shinitzky
Founder, *EQUUS* and *Dressage Today*

PART ONE

LEARNING TO EVALUATE CHARACTER

CHAPTER ONE

Introducing Equine Personality

I first became interested in the question of equine personality when I was 12 years old. I was raised on a farm in rural Alberta, Canada, where I rode my chestnut mare Trixie to school every day — not just for the joy of it, but because she was the only transportation available.

Trixie was definitely a horse with her own mind. One day when I was late for school, she decided she didn't want to head down the road without the accustomed company of my cousins' horses. With little ceremony, she bucked me off onto the road and trotted back home on her own, giving me my first lesson in dealing with equine "smarts."

Both of my grandfathers were gifted with extraordinary intuitive, practical and psychological knowledge of horses. My grandfather Will Caywood, who had a profound influence on me, was a romantic figure. As a young man at the turn of the century, he had been a jockey, riding the "Sunshine Circuit" from Chicago to Florida. In 1902 he was taken to Russia by an Austrian count and trained in the stables of Czar Nicholas II. There, horses trained by him won races with such amazing consistency that in 1905 he was awarded a prize as Russia's leading trainer at the Moscow Hippodrome racetrack.

Years later, I too went to Russia to teach my equine training and riding methods at the Moscow Hippodrome. It was a wonderful experience, like coming full circle, to stand in the same huge arena where he had once been, and very touching to find that his name still opened doors and hearts in Moscow's equestrian world.

The secret of Grandfather's success, he once confided to me, was the highly personal relationship he and his grooms had with each horse. First, he never raced a horse unless it "told" him that it was feeling really good and ready to win, and second, all the horses in his stable were "rubbed" by hand for a full half hour after being groomed. The groom would go over every inch of the horse's body with a firm stroke.

My grandfather's understanding of horses influenced my life as I grew up. At the age of 12, I would stand and watch the behavior of a herd of horses, trying to sense and study their different personalities and idiosyncrasies. I had grown up hearing folk wisdom about how the different shapes of horses' heads indicated various character traits, so when I saw an advertisement for a booklet by Professor James Beery that promised some basic information on the subject, I sent for it, reading with interest how a Roman nose might imply stubbornness and small eyes might indicate meanness.

In my early teenage years, I spent all my after-school time at Briarcrest Stables in Edmonton, where I trained and rode horses for five years. Briarcrest was a training facility known particularly for its success in showing hunters, jumpers and hacks. There, my theories on personality were put to the test every day by my having to deal with different types of equine temperaments. The stable was run by Alice Greaves Metheral, known for her ability to select and train excellent hunters and jumpers. Each Tuesday evening, I attended her lectures on all aspects of horsemanship, expanding my understanding of equine personality and learning how conformation affects not only a horse's physical balance, but his emotional and mental balance as well.

Over the years, my grandfather's wisdom continued to inspire me. In the 1960's he lived with us for a time at the Hemet Thoroughbred Farm, an equine breeding center my husband, Wentworth Tellington, and I had established at Hemet, in the rolling hills of Southern California. We had 80 Thoroughbred brood mares, a band of 20 Arab brood mares, four stallions standing at stud, several sleek Siamese cats, a collection of barn cats, and a family of brindle Great Danes.

Went and I would sit with my grandfather Will at the kitchen table, listening spellbound as he told us about the herbal remedies he used on his horses, his massage techniques, and, particularly fascinating to me, his method of evaluating personality by analyzing a horse's swirls, a system taught to him in Russia by his Gypsy translator.

The art of personality analysis is an ancient one, traditional in a number of cultures that held horses in high regard as individual beings. Interestingly, the Gypsies of Europe and Asia, renowned for centuries for their special relationship with horses, used a method of personality analysis also employed by those great equine experts of the North African and Arabian deserts, the Bedouins.

My grandfather's Gypsy translator introduced him to this age-old tradition, teaching him a system that uses the placement and number of swirls on a horse's head as specific indicators of character and temperament. Body swirls are a different matter, however, and I don't remember a discussion of them.

In 1964, Went and I moved to Badger, California, to found

the Pacific Coast Equestrian Research Farm, a study center providing information on all aspects of equine care, including management and training.

Still fascinated by my grandfather's swirl theories, we decided to conduct a survey to determine if there was any validity to this system of analysis. Because we were writing a syndicated column for *Western Horseman* at the time, and also because of our extensive international equine affiliations and global newsletter, we were able to gather information on 1,500 horses from nine different countries, including the United States and Canada.

In our questionnaire, we asked each recipient to note the number and placement of swirls on their horses' heads, and also to give us a description of behavior, general attitude and any problems encountered. We correlated the results and found that they tallied uncannily with what we had learned from my grandfather Will. For an extensive review of what our survey revealed see page 38.

In the early 1970's I began lecturing on personality analysis, and was amazed at the popularity of the lectures and the hundreds of requests that poured in from people asking for evaluations of their horses. It wasn't until 1975, however, that I discovered the remarkable fact that not only could you analyze equine personality, you could actually influence it.

Over a 25-year period of working with horses I had developed a method of training and riding which stressed communication and cooperation between horse and rider rather than the use of force and dominance.

I went to Europe in 1972 to teach my method (later formalized as the Tellington-Jones Equine Awareness Method or TTEAM) when I read about a course of studies given by an Israeli, Dr. Moshe Feldenkrais. Moshe, a celebrated physicist, athlete and master of martial arts, discovered his pioneering system of mind-body reintegration from personal experience. Old soccer injuries to his knees flared up, so his ability to walk became severely affected.

Determined to reeducate his legs and body, he worked out a program that would bypass the habitual way he had once moved and would instead utilize every conceivable alternative motion available, right down to the most minute and subtle flexing of a muscle. In two years he was walking again. He had discovered the theories and practices that eventually would help not only those with paralysis and functional impairments, but anyone who wanted to reach his or her fullest physical and mental potential.

His techniques, known throughout the world as "Awareness Through Movement," and "The Feldenkrais Method of Functional Integration," are based on the following ideas.

As we develop and learn to function in and enjoy the physical world — to walk, talk, dance and ride horses, for instance — habitual patterns of neural response are laid down between certain brain cells and certain muscles. For example, if we learned to walk in a slumped way, the body will be programmed to continue to walk that way. If we learned to speak English, our mouth muscles will automatically be held differently for speech than if we had learned French.

The parts of the brain that are so programmed are the only parts we later use for those specific functions. Moshe Feldenkrais, however, developed a system of gentle, non-threatening movements and manipulations that, because they are non-habitual, awaken new brain cells and activate unused neural pathways. The body's stored bad habits as well as those patterns formed in response to tension, pain and fear are broken, releasing the "cramped" emotional attitudes that go with them. Now, new choices are possible and with new choices comes a new ability to learn — coupled with a renewed self-image. The purpose of his work, Moshe often stated, is to give people means to fulfill their highest potential, whether physical, emotional or intellectual.

Studying with Dr. Feldenkrais was a revelation for me, like the feeling you get when you suddenly discover the key to a puzzle you've been working on. I realized that Moshe's ideas were every bit as applicable to horses as they were to humans. If, by using his techniques, a horse's physical or emotional difficulties could be worked with and changed, then maybe what we see as "equine personality" is something that is not "written in stone."

For years I had believed, as do so many people in the equestrian world, that the way a horse is born is essentially the way he is going to stay. I'm sure we've all heard comments like "well that horse is just sour," or "high strung and flighty," or "hopelessly stubborn." While there may be some truth to these basic evaluations, what I learned from Moshe Feldenkrais, and what so radically altered my own way of looking at horses, is that though we can't change the given of genetics, we *can* change what we perceive to be "personality."

The *Random House Dictionary* defines personality as "the embodiment of a collection of qualities; the sum total of the physical, mental, emotional and social characteristics of an individual, the organized behavioral characteristics of an individual." There are many aspects to this definition other than genetic givens, and it seems clear to me that the individual personality of any creature isn't a fixed "thing" at all, but more like a kind of continuous dance of communication that goes on between an individual and the surrounding world.

It's been my experience that many of the behavioral characteristics we attribute to personality problems in the horse actually come from discomfort in the horse's body. In some cases this comes from tension that is inborn, in some cases tension that arises from any number of external causes, such as lack of exercise, inappropriate feeding, cramped stabling, or lack of companionship.

For instance, a horse may be reacting to discomfort or pain caused by poor conformation, or again, behavior that is termed "resistant" or "unwilling" may not be a character flaw at all, but may be caused by a saddle that doesn't fit, a riding position that is painful to the horse, or a rider who demands performance that the horse cannot physically deliver. Sometimes, too, the rider may be transmitting confusing or unclear signals, creating a situation in which the horse winds up being labeled a "stubborn" personality.

And then of course there's the additional factor of how we ourselves interact with our horses — how we perceive them. Sometimes the very fact that we expect a certain kind of bad behavior from a horse sets up a self-fulfilling prophesy; the horse reacts to our own tense attitude by mirroring back our expectations.

When we misunderstand a horse's personality, we are in effect creating a case of mistaken identity. But when we break our old habits of perception and use new ways of "seeing" and judging, we are able to bring out the very best in our horses — and (wonderful bonus) new dimensions in ourselves, too.

Learning about our horses is learning about ourselves as well, seeing how our own personalities mesh or clash with the horses we choose to ride or train. I've been amazed to realize the importance of matching horse and rider. When a mismatch happens it can be like a difficult marriage; if the personalities are disharmonious, no one gets much satisfaction, communication or joy out of the situation.

On the other hand, just because a horse continues to act in a way that is frustrating doesn't necessarily mean that he is unsuitable for the rider, or that the trainer is doing something wrong. Instead, it may be that the horse is not appropriate for a particular discipline, or again the problem may be a quirk of personality that, once understood, can be overcome.

To me, one of the great advantages of knowing how to evaluate personality is how helpful it can be in figuring out just such situations.

I like to think that reading character is a bit like being a detective. A detective begins by using sound investigative techniques to come to certain conclusions. Then finally, in a flash of intuitive insight, all the clues "add up" and the mystery is solved.

My hope for this book is that it will serve as a step by step practical guide, giving you a fresh way to look at horses, a way to judge them with a radically new vision with an eye that is trained to read the meaning behind the features of the head, that can decipher the clues that reside in the conformation of the body, and decode the significance of behavior.

I hope, as well, that it will help you to develop, trust and use your intuition, tuning you in to the universal language of the heart, and reminding you of how, in the first place, you came to love horses.

CHAPTER TWO

Understand Your Horse as an Individual

As I'm sure you know, there's a whole lot more to riding than just getting on your horse and seeing how flawlessly you can sit, how perfect your horse can be on the bit, and how well he can perform at the walk, trot and canter.

There's a depth of relationship that has drawn humans to the love of horses throughout the centuries, a mythic love that we celebrate in story, art and memory from Pegasus to Secretariat, from Alexander the Great's Bucephalus to Walter Farley's *The Black Stallion*, from the classic horses that prance across the ancient frieze of the Parthenon to the many images of horses our own culture employs to speak to us of freedom.

I remember how magical horses were to me when I first began to ride, and I believe many people feel that same sense of inspiration in their initial encounters with them. When you look back to your own early experience, wasn't there a special exhilaration about it, a love and appreciation of horses that came straight from the heart?

Often, however, as you progress and become "serious" in your training, the warm communication of this initial connection gets buried under abstract theories about horses and riding. The simple joy of relating to your horse gets lost in the demand for technique, performance and perfection. It becomes harder to see a horse as a living fellow being, and not merely as something to be mastered.

Most traditional equine training emphasizes ideas and practices that, in my experience, spring more from our own fearful reactions to horses than from true responsiveness and understanding.

Generally, we are taught that to control a horse we must dominate it, that horses are usually not very intelligent and must therefore be trained by constant repetition, that to touch horses too much "spoils" them, that "resistant," "stubborn," "lazy" or "aggressive" behavior is a reflection of personality traits that are best dealt with using force and domination.

But in my experience, when we recognize horses as individuals, each with a different rate of learning, we can adapt our training methods to maximize and even expand learning ability. Inspired by my four-year study of the human nervous system with Moshe Feldenkrais, I developed a system of training called Tellington-Jones Equine Awareness Method referred to as TTEAM and The Tellington Touch. The exercises we call TTEAM (Chapter 9, p. 149) have been specifically designed to stimulate a horse's problem-solving abilities and coordination. In using these methods, you'll find that you can actually improve a horse's capacity to figure things out, to think, to act with intelligence.

But what is intelligence? My teacher Moshe Feldenkrais loved to paraphrase something Einstein once said. "Intelligence," he would tell us students in his intense way, "is measured by the ability to adapt to changing situations."

Only recently have we begun to understand that animals really do have intelligence. Gradually, new perceptions of animals are coming to the fore. *Newsweek Magazine* in a May 1988 cover story entitled "How Smart Are Animals?" reported that:

"Creatures as different as pigeons and primates are dazzling scientists with their capacity for thought. Comparative psychologists have gone from wondering whether apes can comprehend symbols to detailing the ways in which they acquire and use them. Other scientists are documenting similar abilities in sea mammals. Still others are finding that birds can form abstract concepts. The news isn't just that animals can master many of the tasks experimenters design for them, however. There's a growing sense that many creatures — from free-ranging monkeys to domestic dogs — know things on their own that are as interesting as anything we can teach them."

Recognizing that horses are individual personalities with individual mental and emotional responses to the world opens us to a new way of perceiving animal intelligence and therefore of influencing behavior. For instance, knowing whether a horse is a slow or a fast learner allows the trainer to choose the most appropriate teaching method. Not only does an intelligent horse need less repetition than a duller one, too much repetition often bores the clever horse, and he will think up ways of "amusing" himself (sometimes by resistance) that his trainer will probably not find equally entertaining.

Understanding our horses doesn't mean we become "permissive" or that we don't use firmness and discipline when required. It means rather that we open the door to cooperation rather than confrontation, an attitude that leads to successful performance so much more quickly, easily and joyfully than does domination through fear or submission. Such a humane viewpoint often has the unexpected side effect of enriching our whole lives.

A case in point: A few years ago, while I was in Germany on a teaching trip, my friend Ulla Tersh von Kaiser asked me to come and have a look at Peroschka, a 12-year-old black Hungarian mare she had just bought for her riding string at the Waldorf school in Uberlingen-an-Bodensee. She had bought the horse three weeks earlier and was terribly disappointed in her. What she had wanted, she told me, was a horse who would relate to the children in the school and really care about them, but this mare had turned out to be withdrawn and unfriendly.

When I first saw Peroschka she was standing with her head in a corner of her stall, her eyes listless, her stance droopy and unresponsive. Looking at her head for personality clues, I saw nothing that suggested a basically unfriendly or phlegmatic character — the indications were actually the opposite, those of a steady, bright and outgoing nature.

It occurred to me that the mare was probably lonely and homesick for her former surroundings and companions. I've noticed that because people are not used to thinking of horses as having emotions, the fact that they might be disoriented in their new homes and missing their prior lives and owners is often not considered.

I suggested that in the afternoons after school a few of the children should visit Peroschka in her stall, not just to groom but to keep her company, to sit with her, talk to her and just spend time being there with her.

The upshot of that treatment was that Peroschka taught the children not only about equine personality, but about the power of empathy. Outstripping even Ulla's fondest hopes for her, she became the most beloved, popular and successful horse in the school stable. Years later, when Ulla tried to retire her, the mare became so unhappy out in the pasture that she had to be brought back home to school and put in light work again.

In another case of a misunderstood personality, the horse in question reacted to emotional stress with aggression rather than withdrawal.

This was an Arab mare whose new owners (they had only owned the horse for a month) had come to the conclusion that she was incorrigibly aggressive and resistant. When they tried to work her on a longe line, she would turn into the middle of the circle with her ears pinned back and attack them. As a last ditch effort before putting her down, they called me.

What I found when I arrived amazed me. The shape of the mare's head did not at all match her behavior. The mare's head was very fine and showed an unusually high degree of intelligence, sensitivity and imagination. What's going on here, I thought — this horse should be a joy. As I examined her further, I noticed that she had a very dejected look to her eye, a look that said, "Leave me alone." It was an expression I'd seen before in the eyes of depressed animals.

I asked the owners to tell me what they knew of her past history. It turned out she had been previously owned by a young boy who was blind. Horse and boy were completely devoted to each other, and by taking patient, attentive care of him when he rode, she had given him the gift of freedom. However, for some reason the boy was forced to sell her, and now here she was, depressed, aggressive and misunderstood.

I decided to try her on the longe line myself. Almost immediately she attacked me, neck snaked out, ears nearly flat against her head. Her present owners had been whipping her for this behavior, but in view of what I knew about her, I refrained from strong-arm tactics and simply stood my ground instead. When she saw that I didn't "scare," she stopped her charge.

Because of the mare's aggressive behavior on the longe line, her owners had not yet ridden her. Suspecting that her behavior might be in reaction to the whip, I recommended that longeing be dropped from her training, and discovered that under saddle, the mare was, indeed, a joy to ride.

After this initial encounter, I rode her for a month, making sure, in the beginning, to acknowledge her loneliness. By taking time with her in the stable and paying extra attention to her, I let her know that new humans were there for her, too, even though she missed her old friend. In a remarkably short time, she proved to be an absolutely phenomenal horse, and was so cooperative that I was able to ride her with only a stiff rope around her neck, which gave her a feeling of trust and freedom.

Her owners thought I was a magician — but the magic did not come from me. It came from my understanding of the horse's basic personality, the comprehension that this was the kind of horse who would do anything for you, but only as long as you related to her as an intelligent being. She was used to being treated by her previous owner as an individual, not just a "horse," and her new owners, like many people in the equine world, were not accustomed to viewing horses in these terms. Since her sense of herself was very strong, she was unwilling to cooperate with people she didn't know or with whom she had formed no bond. Her immediate response to domination or punishment was aggressive resistance.

One of the really important ways in which personality evaluation improves horsemanship is as an aid in preventing such misunderstandings. The way a horse reacts mentally, emotionally and physically to the primary behavioral triggers of pain (emotional or physical) and fear has everything to do with the kind of individual he or she is. Knowing your horse's innate tendencies allows you to correctly evaluate and even predict behavior under a variety of circumstances, and to adjust your training methods accordingly.

There are four ways in which horses (and humans) spontaneously react to misunderstanding, fear or pain: with the impulse to flee (escape), to fight (aggression), or to freeze (immobilization) or to faint (unconsciousness). I like to call these reflexive responses the four F's.

Over and over again in my experience with horses and other animals, I find misunderstanding, fear and pain at the root of learning or behavioral problems. While all creatures in the human-animal family react with the four F's, these reflexes are particularly obvious in horses because of their size and sensitivity, and because of the special demands we place upon them. In the wild, horses will normally flee from threat rather than stand and fight, but in their restricted domestic role, situations they experience as fearful can trigger any of the four reflexes, depending on the personality of the horse and the circumstances.

Some individuals, like the Arab mare, turn their fear and pain into "fight" — biting and kicking, and when pushed to the point of feeling cornered, attacking. Others, when put in a position where they can't escape being beaten or threatened, either "freeze," locking all four legs and refusing to move, or, in extreme cases, lie down and simply give up ("faint"). I've seen horses who are so afraid of loading into a van that, even after being whipped extensively, they actually collapse on the ramp — or faint — rather than be forced inside.

In the literally thousands of cases we've tracked and in my personal experience, too, I've found that there are definite correlations between certain indicators on a horse's head and what type of reflexive reaction will occur. For instance, according to some neuro-biologists, there is a chemical reaction in the brain that acts like a trigger when an animal feels threatened, setting off either the flight or the fight reflex. Looking at a horse's head will give you a good idea of which response will be more likely.

For example, a dish-faced horse (page 19) would have a tendency to the flight reaction, while a horse with a quirk bump below the eyes (page 23) would be more likely to fight. If a horse with a pronounced Roman nose is treated aggressively, he will probably react by fighting back.

There are exceptions, of course. Some dish-faced horses, when denied their initial impulse to flee by restrictions that make them feel helplessly cornered, will switch into the fight mode, sometimes continuing to battle their handlers until they drop.

The freeze reflex is one I've often seen, even in a straight-profiled horse (page 19) who is cooperative but simply doesn't understand what it is you're asking of him. Such a horse will neither fight nor attempt to get away; he will simply freeze and give up all action.

I find the freeze reflex fascinating because it is so often misunderstood, not only in animals but in humans as well. Actually, it was during my work teaching disturbed and learning-disabled children through hippotherapy (therapy through riding) that I first became aware of how this response functions.

One day I read a paper written by Dr. Annabelle Nelson, a noted psychologist. Her treatise was concerned with the limbic portion of the brain — the part that, in the simplest terms, governs emotion, metabolic function, motivation and intuition.

According to Dr. Nelson's thesis, the limbic system either enhances or inhibits learning ability, depending on the emotional state of the learner. An emotional state like fear cues the limbic system to shut down the body's responses, while happiness and confidence stimulate the limbic system to allow a greater range of response.

So, I thought, when kids are in a classroom situation that makes them feel inadequate, they can't learn because their fear actually *physically* "freezes" them.

It's the same reflex, I realized, that makes a rabbit turn to stone when chased by a predator, an actor go mute with stage fright, or a terrified horse stiffen all four legs and refuse to budge.

The faint reflex is one that I've witnessed mainly in trailer loading situations. From what I've seen, most horses who are resistant to loading are either nervous, have had bad experiences loading, are claustrophobic, or have never been taught how to go into a trailer through specific exercises. Sometimes too, they fear the hollow sound of their hooves on the ramp. The first reaction for such horses seems to be one of flight, trying to get away by half rearing and spinning. When they find they can't escape, they go into the next phase, which is to freeze, and if whipped extensively, sometimes simply give up and lie down.

I saw one case like this where a lip chain was used under the upper lip, causing the horse so much pain that in the end she simply fell down and lay there in what appeared to be a catatonic state.

More often than not, handlers misinterpret the four F's, reading them as a horse's intentional attempts to resist the trainer and enforce his own will. Usually, however, what is really happening is that the horse's consciousness is on hold. His breathing has become inhibited, certain impulses in his brain have actually shut down, and he is, so to speak, on automatic pilot.

Often, such misunderstandings about motive lead us to jump in with our own reflexive responses. We become frustrated and then aggressive ourselves, and so the mutual stress and impasse continue in a kind of vicious cycle.

In my experience, action based on mutual understanding rather than on reaction is not only more effective, it actually permits the horse to learn, meaning he will not be compelled to repeat the undesirable behavior under similar circumstances. When you give your horse a chance to clearly understand what it is you're asking of him, you are, in effect, interrupting both his and your own cycles of reflexive response, and the way will be open for the horse to accomplish real learning.

Misunderstandings of a horse's reflex reactions can come in many guises. Take a young horse, for instance, first time mounted and unprepared to move forward from a voice command, signal or stroking. The rider mounts and the horse just stands there and freezes. I've read books where such a horse is described as

having a spoiled and stubborn personality. I've talked to trainers who tell me that when a horse refuses to move he is simply
deciding to dominate and take control.

When a horse won't move forward in this situation, the solution of many riders is to spur or kick him, at which point the
horse will often blow up and buck. He is then branded as aggressive, willful and resistant. I don't think this is true — I believe he has been holding his breath and then explodes into the
flight mode. The rider then punishes the horse, exacerbating
the problem.

Such a response doesn't indicate bad character — it is simply
the way in which those particular individuals are programmed
by nature to cope with fear and pain. And here's the good news:
Reprogramming is possible.

Another common misreading of personality is to label a horse
as "high strung," "nervous," or "willful" when he is actually reacting to tension, pain or discomfort in the body. I know from
personal experience how sensitive and irritable pain can make
me feel, and I'm sure you probably do, too. Since a horse can't
tell us about his pain, we can too easily assume that his behavior
stems from a personality problem.

If you analyze a horse's head and body and find no propen-
sity for such nervous behavior, physically check the animal for
areas of pain, tension or sensitivity (page 161).

I first realized the major relationship between pain and personality when I was living in California in 1975. I've never for-
gotten the experience, because although I'd already been working with horses on a daily basis for 30 years, it was a revelation.

A student had asked me to go with her to look at a pleasure
horse she wanted to buy for trail riding. We drove to a stable in
San Jose, enjoying the tawny hills and the spicy smell of euca-
lyptus on the way. The horse, a nine-year-old Thoroughbred
gelding, was brought out into the arena, and my student
mounted him and proceeded to put him through his paces.

I didn't need to see more than two rounds — the horse had
his ears pinned back and his head up and was wringing his tail
the entire time my student was on his back. "Thank you very
much," I said to the owner, "but this is not the kind of horse we
had in mind."

"I don't understand it," she replied. "He isn't usually like this."

Though I knew that many people who are trying to sell a horse
are liable to say anything to make a sale, I decided to ask a few
questions anyway.

"Well," I said, "if he doesn't usually do this, could you have
done anything different with him in the last few days that might
have caused him to change his attitude?"

She looked thoughtful. "I did take him out on a trail ride two
days ago," she said. "He hadn't been out for months and he was
nervous and jiggy the whole time, so I turned his head to one
side to keep him back."

We unsaddled the gelding and I ran my hands over his entire body, discovering that not only did he have a really hot spot on his neck, but his back was very sore to the touch. I stepped back and then suddenly, as I stood looking at him, a brand new realization clicked into place in my mind: Wait a minute, I thought, what appears to be a personality problem can actually come from pain or discomfort in the body. This means that if you can relieve the pain in the body, you can change the personality.

I could hardly believe the implications of this understanding. In 1965 my husband and I had written a monograph called *Physical Therapy for the Athletic Horse.* We had spent years working on horses with massage and physical therapy to speed recovery after hard work. As a NATRC (North American Trail Ride Conference) judge, I had checked many horses, but never had this concept crossed my mind — never had I realized that pain and personality could be inextricably bound together.

It was a whole new way of looking at horses.

Since then I've seen over and over again the transformative power of understanding. Once we begin to see our horses as individuals, our ways of riding and training become flexible and new possibilities open for us. As we begin to lose our fear of being kind to a horse, we discover that anxiety and tension are released.

Instead of holding our breath, we can let go and we "breathe easy." With the knowledge that kindness doesn't automatically mean loss of watchfulness, judgment or control, we realize that we can allow ourselves the great pleasure of befriending our horses.

We begin to see such understanding expand into other areas of our lives; we tend to be less inflexibly hard on ourselves as riders and as trainers; we bring greater patience and thoughtfulness into our relationships with our children, our loved ones and our friends. Something enlivening enters and warms our cerebral concepts of discipline and ambition, something that adds both sympathy and clarity — I like to call it heart.

CHAPTER THREE

The Elements of Analysis

Evaluating equine character is an art — and like any aspiring artist, to become a virtuoso you need to learn, practice and master the basics first. Once these basics come to you as effortlessly as your own breath, you'll find yourself "seeing" horses with completely new eyes, as though you'd put on a pair of magic glasses.

Shape and size, profile and posture become indicators. The features of the head, swirls, proportions of the body — all will gain a new meaning, all will come together to paint for you an outline of character, a portrait of personality. And as you learn, perhaps you'll be as astonished and impressed as I am by the multitude of differences, by the infinite and subtle variations that life continually weaves around the theme of "horse."

Your horse's head is a major expression of his personality. Learning to recognize the meaning behind the placement, shape and size of ears, eyes, profile, forehead, nose bone, nostrils, muzzle, jowl, mouth, lips and chin is one of the major keys to understanding his nature. Here follows a reference guide delineating what various aspects of the head indicate in terms of personality, as well as an explanation of the locations and meanings of swirls. Finally, there are some exercises to help train your eye to look at horses in a new way.

Reading the Head

The Profile

Generally speaking, a straight face is uncomplicated, a dish-face shows sensitivity and sometimes timidity and a Roman nose usually indicates boldness. However, these indications should be read along with the other features that are prominent in the head.

A Roman-nosed horse can be an excellent performance horse depending upon his eye. Many of the original Lippizaners from the Spanish Riding School had Roman noses (before Arabian blood was introduced). They had large soft eyes, similar to the most successful Argentine polo horses who also have Roman noses and large eyes. Some of the most famous bucking horses, on the other hand, have been small, pig-eyed, Roman-nosed types. I have known many excellent, hardworking school horses with Roman noses and medium-sized, intelligent eyes.

I would not suggest a dish-faced horse for a polo pony, and an Arabian with a straight profile is usually better for performance such as endurance riding than one with a dish face.

The dish face has been read in a number of different ways by different cultures and breeders. Let's take the Arabian horse, for example. It's interesting to note that Lady Wentworth (the late British author of *The Authentic Arabian* and many other books, and a well-known breeder of Arabians) favored a dish face and bred horses for this characteristic. But, according to Mary Gharagozlou, a prominent Iranian judge and breeder, the old-time Bedouin breeders of Arab horses did not find an extreme dish face acceptable, and sold all such horses to Europeans! And, in some of the other countries that breed Arabians, Poland and Russia, for instance, the majority of successful Arabian race-horses have straight faces.

In my own experience, a dish face on other breeds, such as Thoroughbreds, Saddlebreds, Quarter Horses, warmbloods (particularly Trakehners), Tennessee Walkers, Paso Finos or Icelandics almost always spells timidity and over-sensitivity. The more extreme the inward curve, the more extreme the tendency. In many cases the horse lacks self-confidence and depends upon a human to give him confidence. When I see a dish face on a horse other than an Arabian, I always pay special attention to the other characteristics of his head.

However, in some Arabians crossed with Appaloosas, Haflingers, or Welsh ponies (as well as some ponies that may have Arabian blood in their backgrounds), the dish face is more acceptable and indicates a softness that can be desirable, depending upon your performance expectation.

1. Straight profile

2a. Dish face

2b. Dish face with moose nose

2c. Dish face, moose nose, and protruding forehead

1. *Straight, flat profile:*
   A horse who is very uncomplicated and learns easily.

2a. *Dish face:*
   A tendency to be sensitive and sometimes timid.

2b. *Dish face combined with a long moose nose:*
   Usually indicates uncommon intelligence and confidence.

2c. *Dish face combined with a moose nose and a bulge between the eyes:*
   Indicates a difficult, often mercurial personality requiring patience and understanding.

3. Roman head

4. Roman nose

5. Moose nose

6. Long nose

7. Long, narrow head

8. Wide from mid-nose bone to jawline

9. Wide, prominent nose bone

10. Slanted forehead

The Profile *(cont.)*

3. *Roman head:*
   This profile bulges out from the forehead to just above the middle of the nose, and then curves downward. Horses with such a head are thought to be stubborn and slow-minded.

   My experience has shown that such horses respond normally when worked with TTEAM training, but if you push them unfairly, they will become very resistant, because they are less flexible and learn more slowly.

4. *Roman nose:*
   This configuration shows up in profile as a slight bulge below the eyes and continues until it reaches the nose. Such horses are often bold, very tough and resilient and seldom seem to get hurt. They are ideal for polo ponies and school horses.

5. *Moose nose:*
   This shows up as a bulge on the lower part of the nose and usually indicates a horse with a strong character, frequently a herd leader. A horse with a dish face that is complemented with a moose nose will be sensitive, but bold rather than timid.

6. *Long nose:*
   When the measurement from the bottom of the protruding cheek bone to the upper lip is longer than average in proportion to the length of the head, and the jowl is small and the head not very tapered, this indicates a slow-witted horse. If there is a large jowl, a broad, flat expanse between the eyes and a tapered jaw line, the intelligence will be higher than average.

7. *Long, narrow head:*
   A horse who is willing and will do what you ask provided you give simple, clear directions. May require more patience than other horses. If the jowl is small and the head narrow between the eyes, the horse may be a slow learner, but will usually be reliable once he has learned the lesson. This head is characteristic of Friesian horses in Holland.

8. *Wide from mid-nose bone to jawline with undefined jowl:*
   Slow learner, inflexible.

9. *A wide or prominent nose bone:*
   May indicate inflexibility.

10. *An extreme slope of the forehead back towards the poll, rarely seen:*
    Usually indicates a resistant personality.

1. Large, round jowl

2. Medium jowl

3. Small, shallow jowl

The Jowls

1. *Large and round:*
   Horse tends to be intelligent and cooperative.

2. *Medium jowls:*
   Average ability to learn (You can bring your horse way beyond average with intelligent education.)

3. *Small jowls:*
   Usually slow to understand. It is possible that smaller space for the wind pipe restricts breathing. This would result in limited athletic ability which in turn creates lack of confidence.

1. Bulge between eyes

2. Bump below eyes

3. "Quirk bump"

Bumps and Bulges

1. *A bulge between the eyes:*
   These horses are usually unpredict-able, often slow learners. Lessons must be repeated often for the message to sink in. Require patience.

2. *A bump (which is rather broad), just below the eyes:*
   Horses with this manifestation may be somewhat inflexible and resistant under pressure.

3. *"Quirk bump" (a small bump several inches below the eyes):*
   May indicate a horse who is predict-able most of the time but who may be given to sudden and inexplicable shifts of behavior. These horses often have trouble with submissive training. With understanding, patience and clear commands, you can overcome their unpredictability.

1. Sloping muzzle

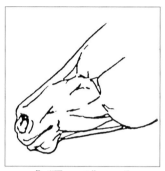

2. Sloping muzzle with moose nose

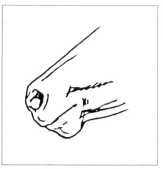

3. Square muzzle

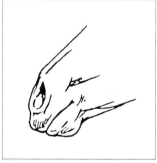

4. Refined, soft muzzle

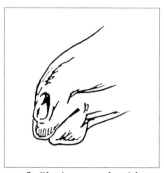

5. "Teacup" muzzle

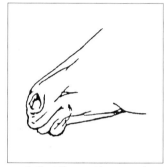

6. Small, complex muzzle

The Muzzle

1. *Sloping muzzle:*
   This characteristic, which I've seen at its greatest extreme in warmbloods, differs from the moose nose in that it slopes sharply from above the nostril to the upper lip. Horses with an obvious sloping muzzle have a strong tendency to test each new rider to see who is going to give the commands.

2. *Sloping muzzle combined with moose nose:* A dominant character.

3. *Squarish muzzle:*
   Tends to signify a stable, uncomplicated nature.

4. *Refined, soft muzzle:*
   Usually goes along with a sensitive personality.

7. Rounded muzzle

5. *"Teacup" nose or muzzle:*
   This British definition (for Arabian horses) came about because the muzzle appeared to be small enough to fit into a teacup. Reflects intelligence and sensitivity.

6. *Small, complex muzzle:* Opinionated.

7. *Slightly rounded muzzle:*
   May be somewhat inflexible and take a little longer to learn new lessons.

1. Long mouth

2. Short mouth

3. Medium mouth

The Mouth

1. *Unusually long mouth:*
   Indicates sensitivity and sometimes a highly active intelligence and an ability to learn very quickly, a combination that can often result in a horse being misunderstood or considered difficult. Horses who learn quickly but are subjected to lengthy routines get bored and look for ways to amuse themselves, behavior which is often erroneously interpreted as "a bad attitude."

2. *Short mouth:*
   This can signal inflexibility and a horse who is slow to learn. It's hard to fit such horses with a comfortable bit, and generally they do better without one, i.e., with a type of hackamore.

3. *Medium mouth (corner of the mouth about even with the top of the nostril):*
   Indicates nothing in particular. Look at other physical characteristics to evaluate personality.

4. *Puffiness or fullness in the area at the top of the mouth:*
   Indicates a stubborn streak. Avoid getting into fights with such horses, as it will only make them more resistant.

4. Fullness at top of mouth

The Lips

1. *Flat upper lip (seen from the front):*
   Generally signifies a horse who tends to be quite independent and single-minded and who tends to mind his own business.

2. *Well-defined or heart-shaped upper lip (when I refer to a heart-shaped upper lip, it's because it resembles the top portion of an upside down heart):*
   A lip like this can be an indication of an expressive, curious and extroverted character.

3. *A mustache:*
   Not a common characteristic. Most horses I've known with a mustache have been friendly "caretaker" types.

4. *Extended upper lip:*
   Sometimes looks like a "parrot jaw" (a conformational fault where a horse's upper jaw protrudes out further than the lower jaw), but actually the teeth are normally set. Horses often extend their upper lips this way when they are concentrating or when they are nervous or uncertain.

5. *Stiff upper lip:*
   This can be a sign of a horse who is introverted and not people oriented.

6. *Flapping lower lip:*
   This can be a sign of nervousness or a horse who is overly sensitive and unfocused. Sometimes, if the lip droops but does not flap, the horse will usually be slow to respond or learn.

7. *Mobile upper lip:*
   Curiosity and the physical need to have contact with humans, mouthing them, for example.

8. *Relaxed upper lip:*
   The upper lip from the front view is not flat across, but gives the appearance of being relaxed because of a slight unevenness and droop below the nostrils. Such a lip implies a relaxed attitude, but can be misleading and must be read in conjunction with other facial characteristics.

9. *Drooping lower lip:*
   Mental slowness.

10. *Complex lip and chin:*
    The lip is clearly separated by ridges and defined as apart from the chin; a complex character is indicated.

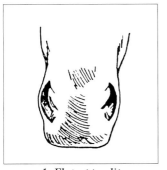

1. Flat upper lip

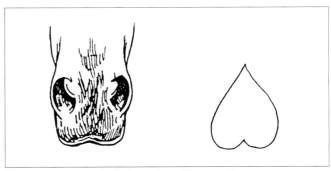

2. "Heart-shaped" upper lip

3. Mustache on lip

4. Extended upper lip

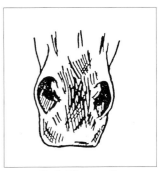

5. Stiff upper lip

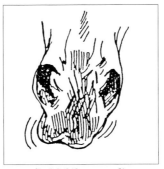

6. Flapping lower lip

7. Mobile upper lip

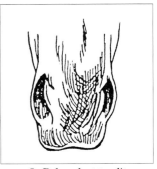

8. Relaxed upper lip

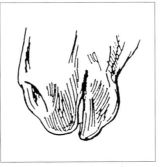

9. Drooping lower lip

10. Complex lip and chin

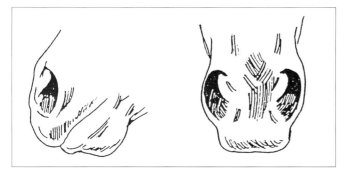

1. Average-size nostrils

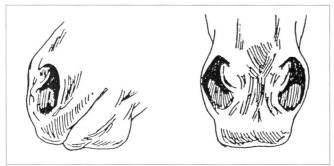

2. Large, open and moveable nostrils

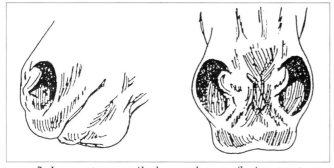

3. Large, open nostrils, loose at bottom, flaring at top

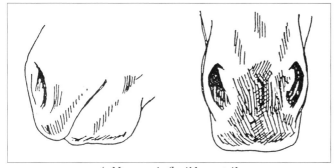

4. Narrow, inflexible nostrils

The Nostrils

There are many types of nostrils. They can be long, short, very moveable or fairly stiff, with thin or thick edges. Horses with large, moveable nostrils are usually more intelligent.

1. *Average size:*
   As wide at the base as at the top; signals average intelligence.

2. *Large, moveable and open (the edge of the nostril will usually be refined and the bottom open):*
   A sign of a nature that is intelligent, interested and eagerly active.

3. *Large, open, loose at the bottom and flaring at the top:*
   Intelligent and an indication of a horse who thinks a great deal. If, however, the skin just above such a flaring nostril is loose, it can frequently indicate a horse who snorts excessively and has a tendency to shy. It is difficult for them to change their ways.

4. *Narrow and inflexible:*
   Shows lack of mental development, or indicates a horse who has difficulty figuring out what is being asked. The nostrils can change as a horse becomes more interested and develops mentally, particularly with TTEAM learning exercises. It's interesting to photograph

nostrils and head shape before training begins to better observe the changes. There will be more changes in young horses as they mature, but even in older horses, surprising changes can often occur. Narrow and immoveable nostrils, when combined with dull, half-closed eyes and ears that don't prick forward, can be a symptom of mental under-development. May sometimes be a sign of nearsightedness.

5. *Wrinkles above the nostrils accompanied by accelerated respiration:*
   May be a signal of pain, or, in the case of older horses with considerable character, it may also be a show of disdain.

6. *Edges of nostrils well defined:*
   Mentally quick, intelligent.

7. *Shapely, fluted at the top:*
   Horses who think a lot. If the top of the nostril has a well-defined shape and is firm, they'll tend to be cooperative if a person is fair and confident. Also, beware if the skin an inch above the top of the nostril is very loose, indicating a tendency to react and snort or shy in new situations.

8. *Large, open and rounded at the top:*
   Alert.

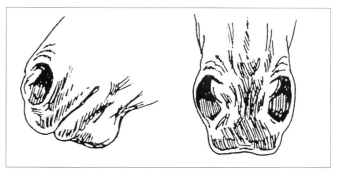

5. Wrinkles above nostrils

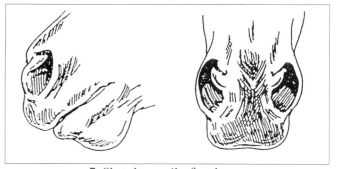

6. Edges of nostrils well defined

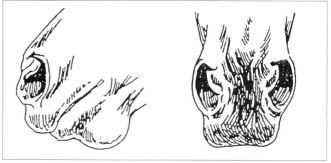

7. Shapely nostrils, fluted at top

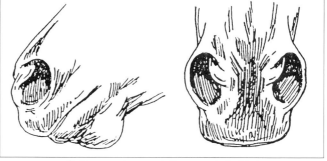

8. Large, open nostrils, rounded at top

The Chin

1. *Round and soft:*
   Signals a nature that can be easy going and uncomplicated.

2. *Pointed and hard:*
   A rock-hard chin can signify a neurotic horse who is somewhat irrational and difficult to change. He can be resistant and often tends to fight the rider. When some horses are upset, their chins will become rock hard. They are not able to learn until the chin softens again. If this is the case with your horse, try softening the chin with the technique described on page 155.

3. *Long, flat, narrow chin:*
   Can indicate high intelligence. Generally is accompanied by a longer-than-average mouth. Often these horses are labeled "difficult."

4. *Double chin:*
   Horses with this type of chin are usually clever.

5. *Complex chin:*
   A chin with a sharply defined separation from the lower lip, or with small ridges. Often indicates complex character.

6. *Medium thickness:*
   Relaxed, with 45 degree angle from the point of the chin to the lower lip: a steady, cooperative horse.

7. *Short and rounded, broad from mouth to point of chin:*
   Can be a sign of a dependable horse.

1. Round, soft chin

2. Pointed, hard chin

3. Long, flat, narrow chin

4. Double chin

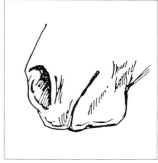

5. Complex chin

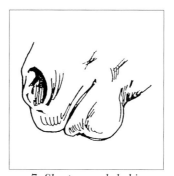

6. Relaxed chin, medium
thickness

7. Short, rounded chin

The Eyes

Learn to distinguish between trusting, depressed, confident, shy, fearful, friendly, cautious or introverted eyes. They will often change and reflect the shift in personality as you begin to understand and work with your horse in new ways.

1. *Large, soft, round eye:*
    Generally indicates a horse who is willing and usually trusts people.

2. *Large, hard, round eye:*
    The expression is proud and distant, what is called "the look of eagles," a look you watch for in a good race horse. A horse with such an eye is a top horse, not easy, but rather proud and independent.

3. *Wrinkles above the eye:*
    An eye that appears triangular with several folds directly above the eye — similar to a questioning frown or a worried look — means that the horse is unsure. If a horse gets such a triangular look when you're working with him, it means he's not understanding what you're asking of him. Don't punish the horse for resisting — instead break the lesson down into easy steps and teach one step at a time.

4. *Tight, round eye with no wrinkles above the eye:*
    Shows a high degree of anxiety and tension.

5. *Medium-size eye:* Average intelligence.

6. *Small eye (if very small is sometimes referred to as a "pig eye"):*
    Such horses are frequently inflexible and slow to learn. They do badly under pressure and become very resistant. A small eye can take on a sunken look when a horse is in much pain. The sunken appearance will disappear when the pain is relieved and the eye will appear larger.

7. *Almond-shaped eye:*
    A cooperative and willing nature. Horse may be introverted and slightly standoffish until he learns to trust you.

8. *Triangular-shaped eye:*
    Average intelligence. Personality will depend on other characteristics.

1. Large, soft, round eye

2. Large, hard, round eye

3. Wrinkles above eye

4. Tight, round eye without wrinkles

5. Medium-size eye

6. Small ("pig eye")

7. Almond-shaped eye

8. Triangular-shaped eye

The Eyes *(cont.)*

9a. *White sclera around the eye:*
This is normal for an Appaloosa or a horse with a blaze.

9b. *White around the eye:*
In solid colored horses, white below or above the pupil that does not change with mood has no particular significance. However, when the white appears or disappears with mood changes, mental imbalance or extreme tension is indicated. When tension is the cause, the white is seen when the horse's head is up and not when the head is down. Some people believe horses with this kind of eye will never be totally trustworthy. In my experience, horses exhibiting white around the eye frequently have body pains that are unknown to their riders, and their pain-instigated behavior is therefore often misread as "crazy."

10. *Hooded, half-closed eye:*
Often withdrawn; slow responses.

11. *Supraorbital deep depression (an indentation above the eye):*
Indicative of a stressful life or a past severe illness. In Canada, I've seen extremely deep depressions in under-fed young horses who spent winters outside, with inadequate feed or shelter, in 40 degrees below zero weather.

12. *Wide between the eyes:*
Intelligent, with an ability to learn quickly. However, this type of horse may use his intelligence to take advantage of an inexperienced rider.

13. *Narrow between the eyes:*
Slower to learn, which isn't necessarily undesirable. It's often even preferable to have a school horse or beginner's horse not be too smart. Once a narrow-faced horse has learned a lesson he usually retains it and can be an excellent worker.

14. *Eyes set high on head:*
Sometimes a little slow to learn.

15. *Eyes set back on sides of head:*
These restrict vision. Horses with these eyes may appear disinterested in their surroundings or, alternatively, be fearful and shy away from other horses or vehicles moving towards them.

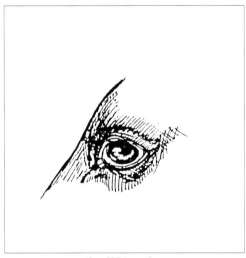

9a. White sclera

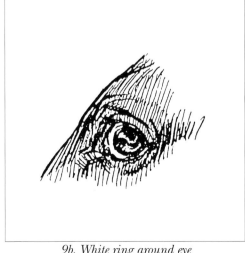

9b. White ring around eye

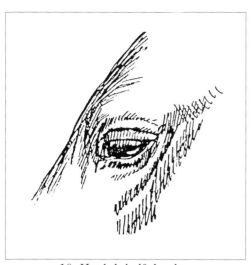

10. Hooded, half-closed eye

11. Deep depression in supra orbit

12. Wide between eyes

13. Narrow between eyes

14. Eye set high, close to ear

15. Eyes set on sides of head

The Ears

Learn to observe small differences in ears. Studying the width, length, shape, set, and distance apart will give you valuable information about character. Keep in mind that the ear description given below should be viewed in relation to what is normal for the breed you are evaluating.

1. *Wider apart at the top than at the base:*
   Indicates steadiness and a tendency to be uncomplicated.

2. *Stand straight up, set wide at both base and top:*
   Horses having this ear set are likely to be energetic and sometimes a little hot.

3. *Set wide apart at the base:*
   Likely to have a good capacity for learning. Steady.

4. *Long ears, narrow space at both base and top:*
   A tendency to be changeable and inconsistent.

5. *Space between ears narrower at the top than at the base:*
   Usually this type of ear is very refined at the tips. These horses are often hot and spirited. Some of the champion Morgan and Arabian park horses and Saddlebreds have these ears which give them animation in the show ring.

6. *Lop ears:*
   This is a sign of great dependability.

7. *Broad shapely ear:*
   Denotes steadiness and reliability.

8. *Broad ear with little definition:*
   A horse who is not going to ask many questions, but will just go on down the road as you ask. Medium learner. Cooperative.

9. *Fine or fluted with delicate definition:*
   Usually signifies intelligence.

10. *Pin ears (very short):*
    Horses with ears like this are often willful.

11. *Tufts in the ear:*
    Often indicates willfulness and inflexibility.

1. Ears wider at top than base

2. Ears straight up; same width at top and base

3. Ears set wide apart at base

4. Long ears, narrow at base and top

5. Ears set narrower at top than base

6. Lop ears

7. Broad ear, flaring out in middle

8. Broad ear with little definition

9. Fine, fluted ear

10. Very short ("pin ears")

11. Tufts in ears

Swirls

Swirls on horses are the equine equivalent of fingerprints on humans. With no two patterns alike, they are like stamps marking each individual's unique identity. In a number of breeds swirl patterns are used as identification for horses: The Arabian Horse Association requires a record of swirls as identification for racing, and the American Quarter Horse Association uses swirls as a means of identification for solid color horses. When Thoroughbreds are registered, part of the procedure is to record the swirl patterns on the face and on both sides of the neck.

A swirl, or whorl, as it is also called, can be defined as a distinctive pattern in the lay of hair on an animal, often having the design of whirling, flexible spokes rotating about a center. It was my grandfather Will Caywood who first drew my attention to them, teaching me that there is more to these odd "cowlicks" than meets the eye.

As I mentioned earlier in this book, during his stay in Russia as the leading trainer for Czar Nicholas II, Grandfather's Gypsy translator taught him how to read equine character by analyzing swirls, a skill that had been passed down among Gypsy horsemen for centuries. Later I learned that the fabled Bedouin horsemen of the desert also placed much significance on the interpretation of swirls, using them as a way of determining the value and price of a horse.

In 1965, my husband and I conducted a statistical survey to define the correlation between facial swirl patterns and locations and certain temperamental and personality characteristics. We sent forms to the international membership of our Pacific Coast Equestrian Research Farm seeking to verify the validity of what some skeptics might dismiss as mere "folk superstition."

Our detailed questionnaire was returned with observations on 1,500 horses. Since that time, I've spent years studying the phenomena in my own equine character readings around the world. The resulting system of analysis is proving to be not only fascinating and provocative, but also truly helpful.

In 1979, in Israel, I visited a ranch overlooking the Sea of Galilee where guests could go riding. I was asked if I would look at a rent-string horse who was so vicious his owner was at the point of putting him down. The horse, a black gelding about 14.3 hands, kicked and bit and was difficult to saddle and mount. He had to be cross-tied and it took two people on either side to lead him.

I asked to see the horse and found that he had a long swirl on the forehead extending several inches below his eyes.

"You know," I said, "I don't believe this is a mean horse. Such a swirl usually indicates a friendly nature. There must be some cause of his aggressive behavior."

When we cross-tied the horse, I examined him and found that he was very sore in his neck and had hot, rubbed spots on both sides of the withers. I checked the fit of his saddle; it was one of the worst I have ever encountered. The pommel sat directly on his withers, and the gullet pressed directly on points below and behind the withers. Pressure on these points caused pain and also affected the horse's diaphragm, interfering with his breathing.

I did body work on the painful areas, using the Clouded Leopard TTouch (page 153). After I had worked on him for one hour, I was able to relieve enough pain that the horse stopped pinning his ears and trying to bite. His owner could hardly believe he was the same animal and decided to give the horse another chance, with a saddle that fit.

Now, if that horse had not had long swirls, I wouldn't have been so quick to think the problem was a physical one, but his behavior was extremely uncharacteristic for the type of swirl he did have, so I looked for pain in his body.

The best way to use face swirls in analyzing personality is to evaluate them in conjunction with all the other characteristics of the horse's head. For instance, a professional rider who lived and worked in Germany saw an article I had written for *Freizeit Im Sattel*, a German equestrian magazine, and wrote to me. She enclosed a photograph of a horse who was giving her a very hard time and asked for an opinion.

She had bought the horse to train in dressage, she wrote, but she was totally frustrated because she could make no real progress with him. He was extremely resistant and unresponsive, and worse than just being discouraged, she was beginning to lose confidence in herself as a trainer.

I took one look at the horse and thought, well, no wonder she's feeling frustrated. The horse had three clustered swirls on the forehead, short ears set close together, very narrow nostrils, small eyes and an extremely short mouth. The ear, nostril, eye and mouth characteristics formed a picture of a resistant horse with a low intelligence, and the three swirls added a factor of unpredictability.

In answering her letter I wrote, "Considering how many horses you have to ride and what you want from this horse, I would suggest you sell him to someone who is intrigued by a complex character and wants a challenge. Look for a rider who has the time, patience and interest to work with a resistant horse."

A few weeks later she replied, telling me she was so relieved to hear that the fault was not with her training. Many people feel like failures when they decide to give up on a horse. I've found that personality evaluation can be very useful in helping riders to make such a decision.

Note: Before you go on to the next sections on the types of swirls and their meanings, let me emphasize that when conducting a personality analysis, swirls must not be read simply on their own but rather as one of numerous contributing factors.

1. Single swirl above or between eyes

2. Single swirl below eyes

3. Long, single swirl

Facial Swirls

1. *A single swirl between or above the eyes:*
   This pattern and position is the standard one displayed by the majority of the horses in our studies and in my observations. It indicates a horse with a generally uncomplicated nature, but there are variations. Sometimes swirls are set a little to one side or the other.

   With swirls set to the left as you face the animal, the horse will tend to be a touch more complicated but still trustworthy. Horses who have a swirl set a bit to the right of center may be less cooperative than those with the pattern in the center or to the left.

   In general, swirls of this sort are less indicative of character than the more complex patterns.

2. *A single swirl several inches below the eyes:*
   I have found that over 80 percent of horses with this configuration are unusually imaginative and intelligent. They like to amuse themselves and can be quite a nuisance. I've known of horses that turned on water faucets, opened stall doors to free themselves and other horses, untied complicated knots, and found ways to escape the pasture.

   These horses are usually of above average intelligence and interesting characters to deal with.

3. *A single, long swirl that may be between the eyes or extend below:*
   Indicates a horse who is friendly and particularly enjoys relating to people. Over the past twenty years I've repeatedly found that when horses with this swirl are unfriendly, it is because they are in pain or have been abused.

4a. Double swirl, side by side

4b. Double swirl, one above the other

4a & b.

Two swirls adjoining, either one above the other or side by side: These can be above, between, or below the eyes and are sometimes set at an angle to each other. The information to be gained by reading this pattern has proven to be of particular value to riders and trainers over the years. Horses with this combination tend to be more emotional and over-reactive than average. They tend to become upset without apparent reason, and at unexpected moments.

When such horses blow up, the best way to handle them is to back off and allow them to settle. Punishing them doesn't help; in fact it usually only aggravates the behavior more and can even bring on more resistance.

I've found that this evaluation holds true about 70 percent of the time. However, a horse with two adjoining swirls can be a great horse. Some of my very best show horses have had this configuration. But generally, horses with this pattern are not ideal for inexperienced riders.

Before I developed the TTEAM method, I usually recommended that horses with two swirls adjoining be ridden only by experienced riders. Now, however, with patience and the TTEAM methods, you'll find you can almost always eliminate undesirable, over-reactive tendencies.

Robyn Hood, my sister and inspiring advisor, raises Icelandic horses. She has observed that Icelandic horses tend to have more double swirls than other breeds. Some of them, she says, do seem to be somewhat emotional, but less so than other breeds with the same pattern.

Robyn has also noticed that Icelandic horses have a lot more swirls in general on different parts of their heads, like the cheeks and the sides of the face just above the mouth. In these horses, the frequency of the swirls doesn't seem to correspond with the complexity of the horse to the same degree as it does in other breeds.

Interestingly, Icelandic lore has it

Facial Swirls (cont.)

that when Icelandic horses have swirls on the neck or crest, they make good swimmers. This is useful in that country with its dangerous rivers and shifting tides.

5a,b & c.

Three swirls close together on the forehead (not up under the forelock): Triple swirls are rare; very few were reported in the survey. However, from my own observations in the ensuing years, I've seen that, in geldings and mares, the triple swirl indicates a complex individual but not an unpredictable one. Stallions, however, are another story entirely — about 80 percent of the stallions I've observed with this marking have exhibited unreliable, often dangerous behavior.

Though most rare, I have seen cases of multiple swirls on the face, and would venture to say that such patterns would tend to indicate complex horses. Many years ago I was a judge at a horse show in California, and in the line-up I noticed a small, liver chestnut mare who had an amazing 16 swirls on her head.

It turned out that she was a very successful junior jumper, but her owner, a 15-year-old boy, was the only one who could ride her. The young man said she had been very difficult to train initially, but now she was very attached to him and would do anything for him.

5a. Triple swirl, one above two

5b. Triple swirl, two above one

5c. Triple swirl, three in line

Here is a photographic selection of seven swirl patterns. Different breeds and horses in different countries demonstrate specific variations in these patterns. Out of 20 horses I observed on a recent trip to Jordan, four had swirl patterns that were new to me. If you run into any unusual swirls, take clear photographs of the patterns or make an accurate drawing, and describe the horse's general behavior. Send all this information to our TTEAM office (see page 179). I would like to collect swirl patterns from around the world and eventually do another survey.

1a & b.

> *Winner:*
> Long swirl extending evenly below and above the eyes. Friendly, interested.

1a. *Winner*

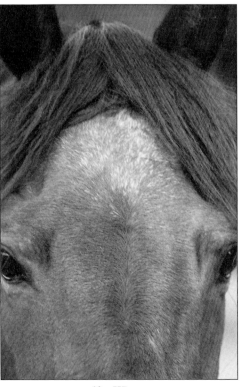

1b. *Winner*

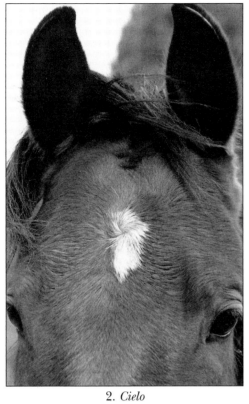

2. *Cielo*

3. *Leia*

4a & b. *Savannah Wind*

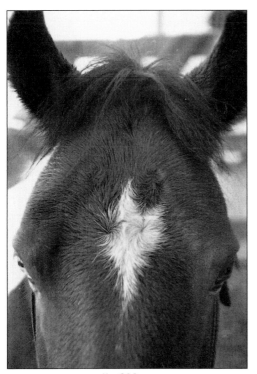

5. Ohlone

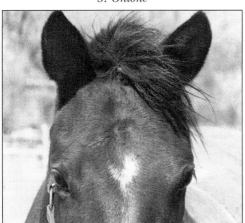

6. Tulip

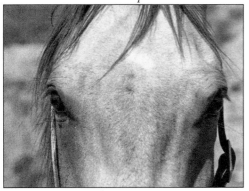

7. Amigo

Facial Swirls *(cont.)*

2. *Cielo:*
   Single swirl set in the middle of the forehead. Generally uncomplicated nature. This swirl pattern indicates less about personality than the more complicated ones.

3. *Leia:*
   Swirl set to the right above the eyes as you face her. Indicates she has a tendency to test the rider and have her own ideas.

4a and b.
   Savannah Wind:
   Small swirl set directly in the middle of the forehead between the eyes. Uncomplicated. Such swirls do not tell as much about character as other, more complex swirls.

5. *Ohlone:*
   Four swirls grouped together just at the top of the eye level. An interesting and unusual character.

6. *Tulip:*
   Two swirls set side by side in the middle of the forehead. In 70 percent of cases, horses with this pattern will tend to react badly in stressful situations. Tulip is probably an exception to the rule, however. Her broad, wide-set ears would indicate stability, mitigating the effect of the swirls.

7. *Amigo:*
   Two swirls set one above the other between the eyes. Can be read as a warning. 70 percent of horses who have this pattern are more sensitive than normal and are easily upset.

Body Swirls

In the swirl survey which we conducted in the 1960's we did not include the study of body swirls, and therefore no hard and fast conclusions can be drawn, but there are a number of interesting beliefs about them. The Bedouins held that a horse with a swirl on one side of the body and not the other would be subject to bad luck. I wonder if this imbalance might indicate a horse who is somewhat unco-ordinated, and that, conversely, horses with symmetrically placed body swirls may be more athletic.

The Bedouins labeled a number of characteristics "bad luck," and perhaps some of these notions had a basis in real-ity. A typical "bad luck" sign was a white sock on the right front leg. Mary Gharagozlou, an Iranian judge and breeder of Arabians, believes this super-stition may be based on the fact that, when riding in battle, Bedouin tribesmen fought with sword or rifle held over the right shoulder, throwing more weight onto the horse's right front leg. Also a white sock extends to a white hoof, and a white hoof is rarely as strong as a black one. Thus horses with such markings who had extra pressure put on them in battle may not have stayed sound, giving rise to the belief that they had bad luck.

In Israel in 1979, I tried to deepen my knowledge of Bedouin equine lore, but I met with no real success. Then, in 1993, Princess Alia al Hussein of Jordan invited me to the Royal International Horse Show in Amman, sponsored by herself and her father, King Hussein. She wished me to in-troduce TTEAM to all the breeders and judges who would be in attendance, par-ticularly those from the Arab countries in the Middle East. To my great delight, I en-countered Mary Gharagozlou and Peter Upton, an Englishman who not only made a specialty of interviewing "old tim-ers" with a knowledge of Bedouin lore but had written several books on the subject.

According to both Peter and Mary, the old-time Bedouin breeders did not care for horses with two swirls on the forehead, and Peter also remembered that they con-sidered swirls high on the neck undesir-able. In speaking of what is considered "bad luck" by the Bedouins, Mary told me that a long, "wheat ear" chest swirl, like the single swirl, is thought to be unlucky. This is, perhaps, because so many horses with this type of swirl behaved in an un-predictable, uncontrollable, even crazy fashion. In fact, she said, the Bedouin people call this pattern "the shredded collar," a term for bad luck, referring to the ancient custom of ripping off shirt collars as a sign of mourning.

"Wheat Ear" or "Shredded Collar Swirl"

Mary has had her own "bad luck" ex-perience with a horse with this "shredded collar" swirl. She fell in love with a mare that she saw for sale and bought her with-out riding her. A few days after she brought the horse home, she went for her first ride. Almost immediately, the mare twisted her head to the side, bolted, and ran full tilt into the side of a building. Horse and rider healed from their inju-ries, and Mary decided to try again. But, once more, the mare repeated the sce-nario, and Mary never rode her again.

Exercises to Train Your Eye

Just as in any other art, personality evaluation calls into play both the conceptual knowledge of the mind and the intuitive knowledge of the heart. An artist uses his learned skill with tools — brushes and paints, clay, pen and ink or whatever — to express his intuitive inspiration.

In character evaluation, you are like an artist, going through a process of integrating what you have learned, combining your analytic observations with flashes of intuitive insight to arrive at your portrait of a character.

I often analyze character from photographs, especially at Equitana, the world's largest international equine trade fair held every two years in Essen, Germany. *Freizeit Im Sattel* has run a number of articles on my evaluations; just before the fair, it usually publishes an announcement that I will be available at the event for those who wish to bring photos of their horses for me to evaluate. So many people come to me with photos that I set aside specific hours each day to evaluate their horses.

While I can read a great deal from photographs of a horse's head, I also ask a rider what is expected of the horse, and inquire about conformation, riding style and equipment; each of these factors is important in the final analysis.

The first step is to look at the horse both in profile and face on. The two different views will give you different information and different perceptions which will add up into a single picture. Just relax and see what jumps out at you. More than likely you'll find yourself forming an immediate, intuitive impression.

This first impression is the backbone of your analysis. Your initial perception may be that the horse is exceptionally friendly, or you might say to yourself, hmmm,

seems a bit slow to learn, or maybe you'll think, if this horse is asked too much too soon, he's likely to resist. With some horses it might be stubbornness that stands out as the focal point for character, with others, intelligence, with still others, gentleness or curiosity.

Now continue your analysis by looking at the expression in the eye, seeking messages of attitude, of mood, of well being or discomfort. Next, observe and interpret the features of the horse's head (profile, jowl, ear set, eye shape, nostril size, mouth length, chin set, muzzle shape, swirls) and write down your findings. Certain characteristics will begin to stand out more than others.

As you practice, you'll begin to see these more prominent features at a glance and you'll find yourself drawing intuitive conclusions from the particular way they relate to each other. For different examples of how this works, see Chapter 4, "Tuning Your Eye," where I evaluate 21 different horses.

I'd like to add here that, because personality is ultimately mysterious, it's possible to be wrong in an evaluation. I've known cases where I have been mistaken, and probably you will find that you, too, make an occasional error.

There is, after all, something ineffable about the heart and mind of a horse, something that can escape our analytic and even our intuitive eye — no matter how astute we may have become — something I like to call his essential spirit.

Generally though, my mistakes have had their reasons. In cases where I've been fooled, it's usually because I was working from a photograph that wasn't characteristic of the horse, or because I lacked information about how the horse was being ridden, kept or fed. Here are

Dusty showing two completely different profiles. Note how his eye is changed.

two different photographs of the same horse (see Dusty on facing page). If I were trying to judge character from these photos alone, I would go wrong. So, the way a horse appears may differ according to his circumstances. For example, he may be out in bright sunlight, which makes him squint his eyes, or again, perhaps his ears are back because he's reacting to another horse. This is why, when someone requests an evaluation, I always ask whether the photograph is a good, accurate representation of the horse.

For a correct evaluation, regardless of whether the horse is in a photograph or standing right there in front of you, it's very important to know as much about him as you can, and to make sure, if possible, that you are seeing the horse at his most typical self.

When I began to compare the photographs of equine heads for this section, looking for distinctive variations, I first traced the profiles of several horses, then the nostrils, eyes, muzzles, the chins, lips and ears. To my surprise and delight, I discovered that tracing them gave me a new perception of the many small differences that in the end determine the overall picture.

Jean MacFarland, who executed some of the drawings for this book, was also struck with the comparisons of the different elements of the head. As an artist she was very excited by the new visual insights these comparison montages gave her.

I believe the process could be very useful and fascinating for you as well, and my suggestion is that you either trace the individual components — profiles and jowl lines, mouths, lips and muzzles, nostrils, eyes, and ears — or take up your pencil and copy them as drawings. In my own experience, tracing the differences made me acutely aware of them, and drawing them developed an even finer sense of the variations.

After sharpening your perceptive eye by practicing with the horses on these pages, take your sketch pad and go out to draw from life. Look at your own horses and others you see around you. Draw the components of each head, compare the differences, and you'll be amazed at how much more you are seeing, how much easier it becomes to intuitively pick up the visual language that allows you to read character.

As another exercise, trace or draw individual parts separately. Observe the difference in length, or flare, or width, for example. Notice the differences in shape, position and set. You'll find that the more you examine these variations, the more natural it will become for you to see them quickly.

Compare the different horses: The ears for instance — the width at the base, the width between the ears, the way each ear is set on the head, the length and breadth of the ear and the shape of the tip, the way the ears tip in or flare away from each other. See how many differences you can spot. Compare each horse for all the other parts of the head.

Then go to the profile: Now that you have analyzed each element separately, the time has come for synthesis. In the profile you can see the overall shape of the head and review how all the pieces fit together, how the various characteristics you have been looking at in isolation relate to each other and to the lumps and bumps of the horse's head.

For profiles, I have included an impression of the personality of each horse rather than a breakdown of the characteristics. You can find such a breakdown in the sample personality evaluations that follow in the next chapter.

Profiles

Begin your study of profiles by placing a sheet of paper over the photo you are working with, so that only the profile line is visible. Then, leaving the profile photos, go to the other photo comparisons of ears, eyes, nostrils and chins. After you have sharpened your eye by studying these, come back to the profiles and focus on the entire head to see how various characteristics combine to create an overall impression.

1. *Almost straight profile, slight moose nose. Square muzzle. Large jowl:*
   Dependable, confident.

2. *Lump between the eyes, slightly rounded muzzle. Small jowl:*
   Complicated.

3. *Quirk bump below the eyes:*
   Usually indicates quirky or unexpected behavior.
   Sloping muzzle and medium jowl:
   Average intelligence.

4. *A hint of a dish face combined with a long moose nose, a large jowl and a delicate muzzle:*
   High intelligence.

5. *Straight profile, large jowl:*
   Self-confident.

6. *A rare and extreme slope of the forehead back to the poll. Large jowl. Sloping muzzle:*
   Potentially resistant and willful.

1

2

3

4

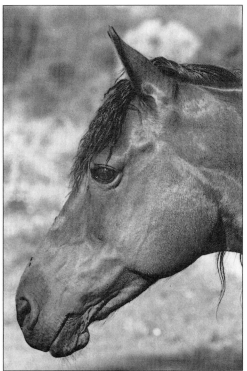

5

6

Profiles *(cont.)*

7. *Flat between the eyes. Dish face. Extreme moose nose. Relatively square muzzle. Large jowl:*
A sensitive, intelligent and complex character.

8. *Very straight profile. Square muzzle. Large jowl:*
All characteristics of steadiness and dependability.

9. *Large lump below the eyes. Moose nose. Small jowl. Wide from mid-nose bone to jawline:*
Inflexible. Slow learner. Potentially difficult.

10. *Straight profile with a small bump below the eyes:*
Some resistance.
Large jowl. Complex, small muzzle:
Usually opinionated.

11. *Straight profile. Sloping muzzle:*
Can sometimes become confused.

12. *Long, narrow head with an unusual and slight convexity of the nose bone plus a small jowl:*
Shows some inflexibility but dependable once directions are understood.
Narrow head and small jowl:
Will make him a little slow to figure things out, but this can be an asset in situations where the horse must trust his rider rather than trying to think for himself.

7

8

9

10

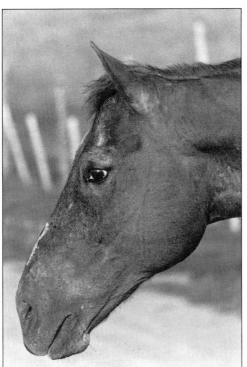

11

12

Ears

1. *Broad, undefined shape. Wider at the top than set at the base. Broad at the base:*
   Dependable.

2. *Exceptionally broad. Wider at the tip than set at the base:*
   A very intelligent and consistent temperament.

3. *Long, narrow ears, straight up:*
   Can be a little slow mentally. Can also be temperamental.

4. *Wider at the tips than set at the base. Fluted tips:*
   Intelligent. Dependable.

5. *Fluted and delicately defined. Quite broadly set at the base:*
   Mentally very quick. Intelligent.

6. *Broad base, wide space between the tips. Nice definition:*
   Dependable.

7. *Short, unusually broad, almost a lop ear in the width between the tips:*
   Dependable, cooperative.

1

2

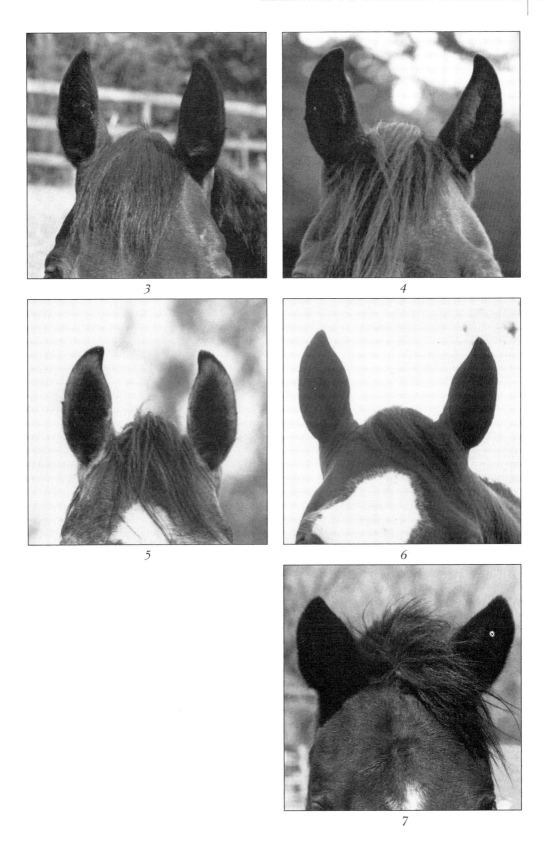

3

4

5

6

7

Nostrils and Upper Lip

1. **Nostrils:** *Average size:*
   Average intelligence.
   Upper lip: *Slightly rounded:*
   Average intelligence.

2. **Nostrils:** *Edges are well defined:*
   Upper lip: *Modified heart shape:*
   Friendly.

3. **Nostrils:** *Fluted at the top, very shapely:*
   Thinks a great deal.
   Upper lip: *Well defined:*
   Intensifies above characteristic.

4. **Nostrils:** *Large with well defined edges,*
   fluted at the top:
   Very intelligent.
   Upper lip: *Prominent heartshape:*
   Unusually curious and extroverted.

5. **Nostrils:** *Average — as wide at the base as*
   at the top:
   Upper lip: *Flat:*
   Both characteristics are indications of
   average intelligence.

6. **Nostrils:** *Large, flared, note well defined*
   edges of nostrils:
   Very intelligent.

7. **Nostrils:** *Average:*
   Upper lip: *Flat:*
   Average intelligence; independent.

8. **Nostrils:** *Unusually narrow:*
   Upper lip: *Drooping and loose:*
   Mentally slow. May be caused by poor
   eyesight.

9. **Nostrils:** *Very refined:*
   Intelligent, curious.
   Upper lip: *Well shaped:*
   Intelligent.

10. **Nostrils:** *Slightly narrow:*
    Upper lip: *Heart-shaped and tight:*
    Curious, a little slow at discernment.

11. **Nostrils:** *Fluted:*
    Upper lip: *Mustache:*
    Usually signifies unusual steadiness.

1

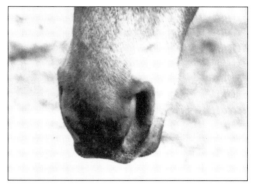

2

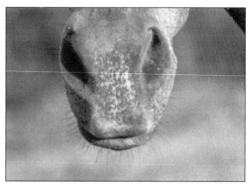

3

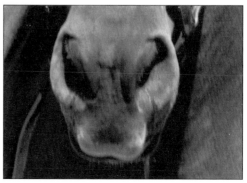

4

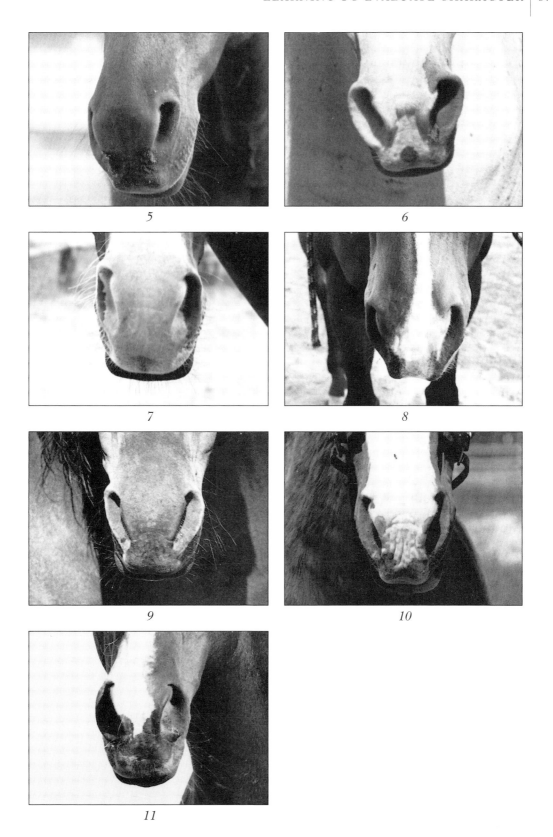

5

6

7

8

9

10

11

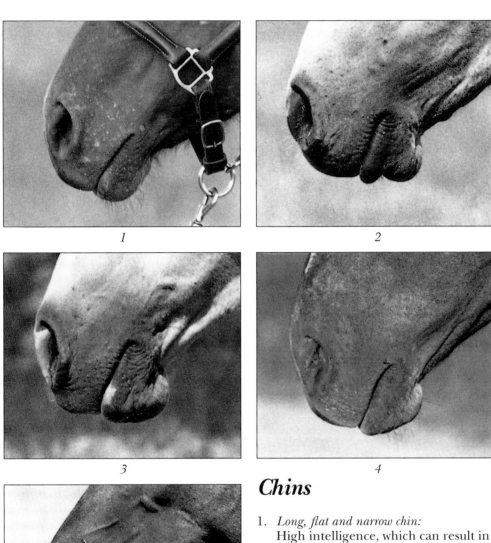

1

2

3

4

5

Chins

1. *Long, flat and narrow chin:*
   High intelligence, which can result in behavior that is often misunderstood as difficult.

2. *A complex chin:*
   Sharply defined separation from the lower lip. Usually, such a chin signals complexity and intelligence.

3. *Short, rounded chin, broad from the mouth to the point of the chin:*
   Usually dependable and not reactive.

4. *Soft chin, average length and width:*
   Average intelligence.

5. *Pointed chin:*
   When the horse with this type of chin becomes nervous or upset, the chin can become hard. The horse will be inflexible and the chin will stay hard until he calms down.

Eyes (Front View)

When the eyes are seen from the front and not in context with the rest of the features of the head, it is extremely difficult to judge their meaning in terms of personality evaluation. I've included a comparison of two front views of eyes here, however, because in observing many hundreds of horses, I've noticed that the more the eye is visible from the front, the more self-confident a horse will be. When the eye is set off to the side of the head, it apparently affects his ability to make visual sense of his world, and therefore can have negative influence on his behavior. Horse No. 2, for instance, has eyes that are hard to see from the front. His owner reports that he often appears not to look where he is going and that he seems to be uninterested and disengaged from his surroundings.

1. *Eyes easily visible:*
   Self-confident.

2. *Eyes set off to side of head:*
   Sometimes can affect horse's visual ability.

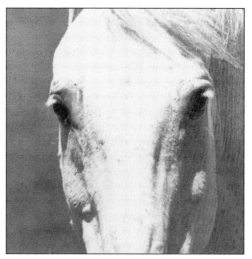

1

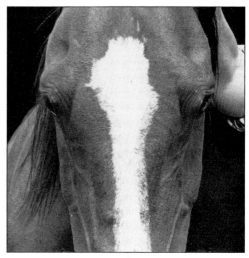

2

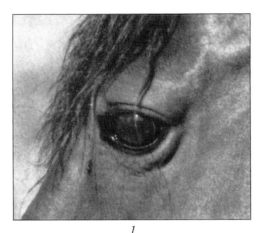

1

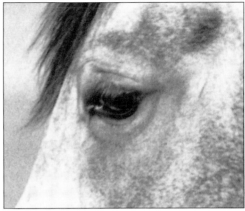

2

Eyes (Side View)

1. *Large, soft and triangular:*
   Very thoughtful, very intelligent.

2. *Slightly hooded, medium size:*
   Introverted.

3. *Small, hard eye:*
   Tends towards resistance.

4. *Medium size eye:*
   Average intelligence.

5. Note carefully the difference
   between this eye and numbers one,
   four and six. Although the eye is
   fairly wide horizontally, it is not very
   high vertically. Almost a human eye
   shape. Very difficult to read.

6. *"Pig eye" (very small):*
   Introverted, a slow learner.

7. *Large eye:*
   Introspective and intelligent.

8. *Appaloosa eye (white around it) with
   triangular worry wrinkles:*
   Wants to please, sometimes becomes
   confused. Since the white around
   the eye is an Appaloosa breed
   characteristic, it can be considered
   normal. White around the eye in
   other breeds often signifies a certain
   wildness.

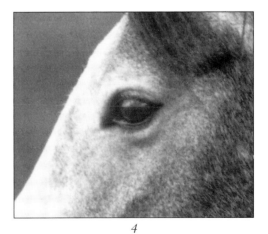

3

9. *Soft, open, clear eye:*
   Interested and hopeful.

10. *Small, sunken eye:*
    Withdrawn, slow mentally, may be
    result of pain.

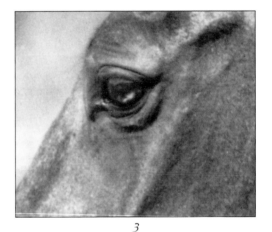

4

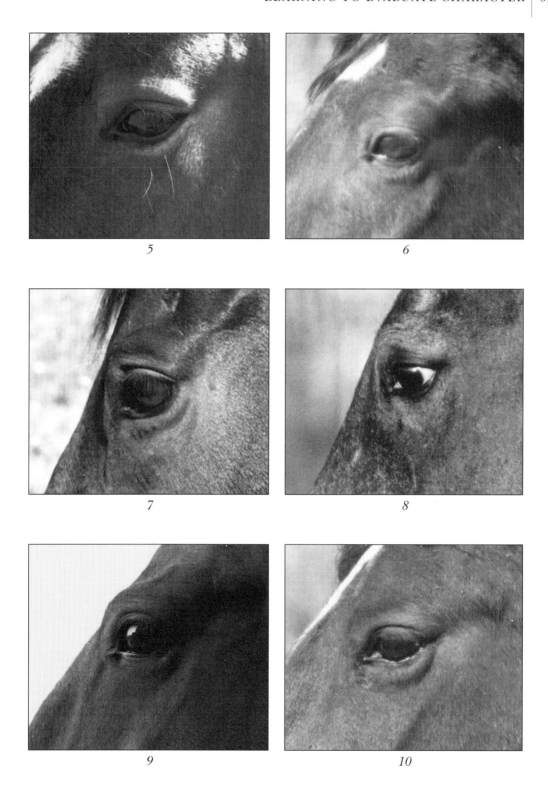

5

6

7

8

9

10

CHAPTER FOUR

Train Your Eye:
Twenty-one Personality Evaluations

I've been examining and evaluating horses for 30 years now, but as I prepared the photos for this book and began to study details and comparisons, I was amazed at how many more details I noticed from intense comparison of many photos. Most people fail to "see" their horses' faces because they are simply not accustomed to observing the nuances.

People who have never owned chickens or cows or goats think they all look pretty much the same, but when you grow up on a farm, you learn to recognize each one as an individual. Yet even this recognition is instinctive — and there is no real conscious understanding of the individuality of each creature until you analyze what exactly you are looking at and what the differences are.

This chapter is meant to sharpen your ability to "see" a horse's head, to interpret the personality characteristic expressed by each separate element, and then to bring these observations together into a meaningful evaluation. It's my hope that by the end of the chapter you'll go out and astonish yourself with what you can see, using your new abilities. You'll probably find, too, that your visual awareness of the world around you will be considerably heightened, adding a delightful new dimension to just "looking."

Abby

ABBY
A 10-year-old Appaloosa mare

I found Abby quite fascinating. In profile, note the extreme quirk bump below her eye, the smallish eye, the long head, the rather small jowl, the large nostrils and the very flat chin and long mouth — I'd say we're looking at lots of potential difficulty here.

Let's analyze these indicators more closely: The prominent quirk bump signifies a horse who will exhibit quirky, resistant behavior at unexpected times; the small eye generally signals an uncooperative attitude; the large nostrils point to a horse with many thoughts going on in her head, often, when combined with a small eye, not in cooperation with the rider; and the long mouthline with the long, flat, narrow chin indicates a great deal of intelligence. Put all this together and you come up with a pretty complex character.

When you add the information you get from the front view, the picture becomes even more complicated. Look at the ex-

treme heart shape of her upper lip (friendliness) and the way the lips on the outer edges protrude downwards, usually a sign of great curiosity. Abby's eyes, although small, have a soft expression and her fluted nostrils underscore her intelligence. These nostrils show that she needs a rider who is fair and confident in order to be cooperative. Her ears are broad, nicely shaped and set fairly widely apart (steadiness). If I hadn't seen the profile, I would have said that she has a very willing, cooperative personality, so I get two different pictures from the side and front — which makes this a very hard shot to call.

Abby's owner really loves her. The words he uses to describe her are all positive; "willing, a hard worker, an excellent trail horse, a great cow horse, easy to handle."

What does this case tell us about equine personality? Abby's mix of characteristics make her a horse who could be either a trial or a sweetheart. Clearly, from her owner's report, she falls into the lat-

Bijou

ter category. What is it that tipped the balance? My guess is that in terms of the "nature vs. nurture" equation, nurture was the deciding factor here. I imagine that whoever started Abby really liked and appreciated her and brought all of her good and exceptional qualities to the fore, thus sublimating the negative aspects in her character. In my experience, if horses with a combination of some or all of these characteristics are dominated, battled or abused when young, they become real fighters. In Abby's case, I believe that the nurturing of all of her good qualities has resulted in making them the dominant expression of her personality.

BIJOU
A 10-year-old Quarter Horse gelding

He has the look of a "packer," a gem of a horse eager to try anything his owner asks and do it safely and willingly. A talented, good-hearted, three-day-event competitor, his owner, Jane Reed, has lessons on

him three times a week and says he takes excellent care of her.

What's outstanding at first glance at both views of the horse is Bijou's straight profile and the flat plane between the eyes, a sign of solid stability. The chin is of medium thickness, relaxed, with approximately a 45-degree angle from the point of the chin to the lower lip. All of these characteristics point to a steady, cooperative nature.

In the side view you can see that his eyes are interested and calm, and from the front, his nostrils, large and open, also indicate a horse who is curious. Curiosity is also apparent in the indentation in his upper lip. Looking at his ears, which are shapely and broad, you once again see that this horse is a good thinker with a stable personality.

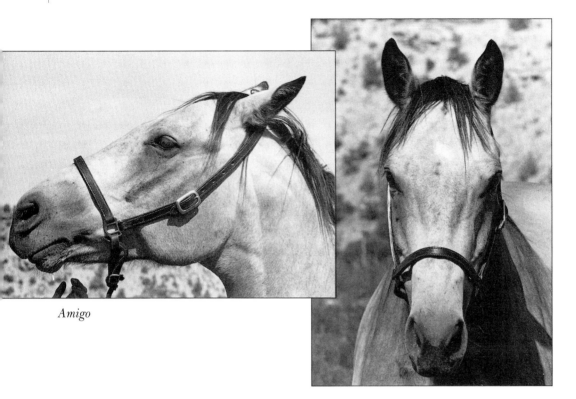

Amigo

AMIGO
A 14-year-old Quarter Horse gelding

Most of the profile photographs we received of Amigo were with his head held high because he resisted all attempts to lower it and was very evasive during the whole photographic shoot.

From the side view, the first thing that struck me was his rather longish head with the eye set quite high. The next thing I noticed was the bump in the profile right by the eye. My attention then went to his lips and chin — in every photo of the several that I examined, his upper lip was extended or the chin was contracted. Since this was not due to a parrot mouth (his teeth were properly aligned) I read it as an expression of concern.

So far, my impression of Amigo was that he didn't trust his environment, that he was inflexible and that working with him would take a lot of patience.

The front view showed me a different aspect of the horse's personality. A sweet eye (when his head was down) with an in-terested, direct gaze; nice, large nostrils; a relaxed upper lip; broadly based ears with the tips wider apart at the top: all the signs of a cooperative personality. If you had no access to the side view, and all you saw was this front angle, you could be fooled by this horse — except, you'll notice, he does have two swirls between the eyes, which indicates that he could, perhaps, be a horse who tends to overreact.

Looking at the overall picture, I could tell that this was a difficult individual, a response that was corroborated when I talked to Jane Reed, who had photographed Amigo for this book. She told me about the difficulties she had in photographing him and also mentioned the different problems his rider and owner, Ann Wells, was having with him. Ann described him as "crazy — he tosses his head when you try to touch it and every time you catch him. He bucks when asked to do things he doesn't want to do, and is unpredictable and stubborn. When you give him a shot, clip his bridle path, worm him or use fly spray, he 'goes up in smoke.'"

Blaze

Amigo does display a certain affection for Ann, despite his difficult behavior. He will follow Ann around the field, and she is the only one who can catch him. My "gut" conclusion about Amigo is that given a chance to develop his self-confidence with TTEAM work, he could develop a trust in his rider that would bring out the best side of him — the qualities I could see in his front view photograph — and turn his personality right around.

BLAZE
A nine-year-old gelding, an Appaloosa-Thoroughbred cross

Looking at Blaze from the front, my first impression is that his ears are set quite a bit wider apart at the top than they are at the base, and also that they are fairly broad and defined — two indications of stability and consistent performance.

On closer inspection, I see that the ears are even more noteworthy than at first glance — the base reaches up about an inch, much farther than usual, before the ear takes its shape. Generally, when you get a highly distinctive and unusual feature such as this in a horse, you can expect to find some equally unusual and unexpected characteristic in his personality.

Add to this the single swirl between the eyes, and nostrils that are average in size with a nice shape and definition (he's not too smart and not too slow), and it would seem logical to think you've got a horse with an easygoing, cooperative personality.

However, when you look at the side view, things get more complicated. Yes, the jowl is large (showing intelligence) and tapers into a squarish muzzle (which usually means stability). The eye, however, is smallish, and above it there is a roundness that slopes back, as though the ears were set back a little on the head, a feature that would indicate difficulty in maintaining concentration and focus. Blaze has a very flat upper lip, which implies a lack of curiosity, even though he is fairly broad between the eyes.

In view of these inconsistencies, I decide to look at the front view again. I no-

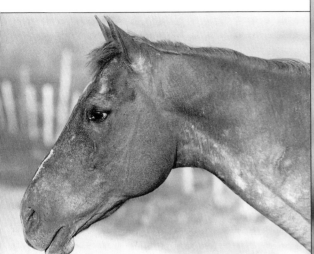

Geronimo

tice that his neck looks somewhat tight, as though it's hard for him to bend it. I surmise that he is probably being ridden in a frame that is hard for him to handle because of his conformation. When you add the irritation of the bodily discomfort that would result from this to the character indications of the small eye and rounded forehead, you get a horse with a resistant attitude, even though his straight nosebone and large jowl would indicate a nature that is easygoing and cooperative.

In talking to his owner, I found out that Blaze was indeed in training for dressage and was considered very uncooperative and difficult to ride. My suggestion was that Blaze's conformation might limit his ability to accept a collected frame, and perhaps both horse and rider would have a more agreeable experience if Blaze were ridden simply as a pleasure horse, and if the owner found a more suitable mount for riding dressage.

GERONIMO
A 17-year-old Appaloosa gelding

Geronimo has been down many roads. He's carried a lot of happy people on his back, running the gamut from barrel racing at 4-H horse shows to working cattle drives. Currently, he's the companion and "baby sitter" of a seven-year-old girl.

Everything about Geronimo's head shows how reliable this horse is — the straight profile, the generous jowl, the clean cut head, the broad ears set wide apart and a little wider at the top than the base, the single swirl, the beautifully defined nostrils, the soft chin, and his trusting, intelligent, thoughtful eye.

Geronimo's personality is as clear and precious as a diamond.

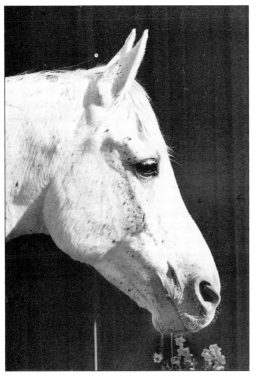

Cymon

CYMON
A 10-year-old Arab gelding

Cymon was traded for $250 and a pair of earrings. He was very well bred: a grandson of Bask, the legendary Polish Arabian sire of many champions, but at the time there were too many of these colts available.

For his first year, when Cymon was still too young to ride, he trotted along with his owner, a marathon runner, on her daily runs through the surrounding mountains. This early work probably contributed to his becoming a wonderful athlete and was a factor in the great friendship that developed between horse and owner. She tells me that his incredible curiosity about everything has earned him the nickname "Sherlock Holmes." Apparently Cymon likes to pretend he's the boss, but at heart he's extremely cooperative.

The first thing that jumps out at me in these photographs is Cymon's dish face and slight moose nose, indicating a combination of sensitivity, boldness and intelligence. In an Arabian, this combination makes for a great deal of character. Notice, too, his square muzzle and pointy chin, meaning that this horse has a lot of thoughts and sometimes holds tension in his chin.

His broad ears demonstrate trustworthiness and stability, and it's interesting to note that an unusual amount of eye is visible from the front view showing a great deal of self-confidence.

Cannonball

CANNONBALL
A nine-year-old Holsteiner gelding

Cannonball, a showjumper, represented the United States in the Barcelona Olympics in 1992. He is ridden by the brilliant rider Anne Kursinski. It's not often that I'm deeply impressed by a horse's personality at first sight, but when I first laid eyes on this horse several years ago in Florida, I said, "Whoooeeeee, here is a major character in the horse world."

His unusual head and nose, the long sweep of his very straight profile, and his strongly pronounced nosebone, from both front and side views, instantly alerted me to the fact that I was looking at a horse with a very powerful, charismatic personality. Here's a horse who will do anything for a rider he likes, but will be very difficult if he takes a dislike to a rider or if the rider attempts to dominate him rather than work with him in partnership. Cannonball is simply too strong a character to be dominated.

He has a large, round eye, a large jowl, and a very unusual length from the base of the jowl to the mouth, which indicates a strong personality and much intelligence. His nostrils are large and well defined, his mouth long and his chin flatish and narrow in shape, also showing an unusually high degree of intelligence. If a rider doesn't acknowledge the intelligence of horses like this, they can be very difficult to handle, but they can be real "wonder horses" for a person who knows how to tap into their potential.

From the front view, one of the first things that hit me was Cannonball's long, narrow ears (compare them to Tulip's). They are set a little close together and straight up, which indicates a horse who can potentially be very difficult. If Cannonball weren't so very intelligent, those ears would signal an almost impossibly temperamental horse. To get along with him, a rider must have fine hands and the ability to sense intuitively every nuance of the horse's feelings at any given moment,

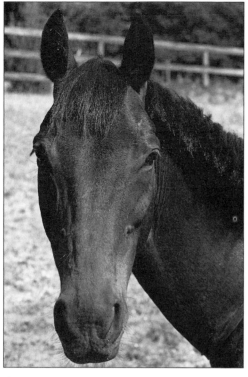 

Dusty

thereby gaining his cooperation by acknowledging his individuality.

Note again in this front photograph how long the head is from the eye to the end of the nose, and the pronounced quality of the bridge of his nose. His lips and heart-shaped mouth show Cannonball's potential for softness, and his large, open nostrils once again demonstrate his intelligence.

DUSTY
A 17-year-old Thoroughbred gelding

Dusty was a successful Pony Club horse, but when he was sold and trained for a higher level of dressage, his owner had difficulty with him.

I think the most unusual characteristic about Dusty is his long and narrow head. Combined with his round and kind eye, this length, exceptional from the jowl down, gives him a sensitivity that can make him extraordinarily empathetic. Looking at the muzzle however, you can see that it slopes off toward the upper lip, meaning he could also have a tendency to test new riders.

His very narrow nostrils indicate some difficulty in figuring out what is being asked of him, and the rather narrow, straight and relatively undefined ears convey a nature that easily turns hot.

Taken together, these indications point to a horse who will go out of his way to help a rider if he trusts him, but if he doesn't, he is a horse who can turn hot and testy.

The front view indicates that Dusty possibly has a ewe neck. If this is the case, his conformation can inhibit his ability to perform. If he's being ridden in a shortened frame that is uncomfortable for him, his sloping muzzle and eyes set high on his head, indicating inflexibility, tell me he could possibly become balky, as he seems to be when asked for a dressage frame.

The little ridges under his chin indicate complexity of character.

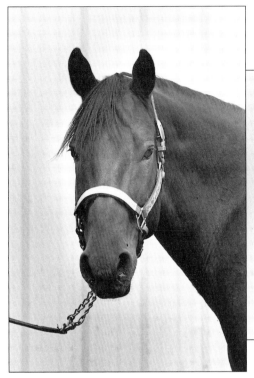

Fax

FAX
A 13-year-old Quarter Horse gelding

Fax was a trail horse until he was nine years old, mostly used for trail riding and for hunting elk and carrying them back out of the high country. Then at nine he started show training, and as a novice he won many ribbons in Western Pleasure, Trail Horse and Showmanship classes.

This is the type of horse that I would pick for an inexperienced adult, a horse who would be kind and take care of his rider.

He has a lovely, typical Quarter Horse head. Note the shortness of the head, the large, very soft eye, the enormous jowl, and the squarish muzzle, all adding up to a confident, safe and cooperative character. His eye is interested, self-assured and wanting to make contact. He also has a medium-length mouth, indicating uncomplicated stability, and his very large nostrils point to a high degree of intelligence.

In the side view, you can see that Fax has a very slight quirk bump on his nose

bone, and just the suggestion of a moose nose, proportions that give him an interesting personality. If these two characteristics were stronger and more dominant, they might mean "trouble," but if you look at the head as a whole, you'll see they are completely outweighed by the other features and merely add a lovely bit of spice to the picture.

This is how, in looking at horses, you develop an eye that can see which features outweigh others. In this case, my eye didn't jump to the quirk bump and moose nose first, but to the dominant large eye, large jowl and squarish muzzle. If I had centered my analysis on the quirk bump and moose nose, I'd have gone wrong.

Looking at him from the front, the impression of this horse's stability is underscored — his ears are medium length, set well apart and are wider at the top. The ear itself is also wide.

The owner tells me that Fax is a horse that anyone can ride. Looking at his head, I can see why.

Jester

JESTER
An 11-year-old Morgan gelding

This is a horse who is changeable and very complex. On the one hand, he has a slight dish face, which means that under the rider he may be timid and shy at common objects, but on the other hand, the bulge on the moose nose, often a signal of a very strong character and "herd boss" type, would indicate that he could be very over-bearing and domineering with other horses in the pasture, and would most likely pose a challenge to his rider.

Compare the difference in muzzles be-tween Jester and Winner (see page 78): In Winner the muzzle is quite square; in Jester it slopes off a bit more under a moose nose, indicating he's a horse who may have a tendency to test a new rider. Compare, too, how Jester's chin and lower lip is more complex than Winner's, with the lip having definition separate from his chin. This complex lip and chin shape often indicates a complicated character.

Jester's large jowl indicates that he is quite thoughtful, and his eye, in the front view, shows an expression of intelligent interest. From the side view, however, you'll notice that he can also be capable of looking right through you.

Jester is certainly very complicated and interesting. He could, potentially, be a difficult horse because of these character-istics. Fortunately for all concerned, his very broad ears lend a stabilizing influ-ence.

Jester's owner says that the horse's ini-tial impulse under saddle was to shy or bolt from something that was frightening him, typical behavior for a horse with a dish face. But before actually putting that impulse into action, he'd often stop and investigate, a behavior pattern that re-flected the boldness and intelligence evinced by his moose nose and large jowl. His owner thoroughly enjoys his complex-ity and the slight dash of mischievousness that adds spice to the whole mixture of this horse who truly is a "Jester."

Kennebec Leia

KENNEBEC LEIA
A 14-year-old Morgan mare

This lovely horse is so alluring her name ought to be "Charisma." Looking at her, I find it very easy to believe that horses think; everything about her head indicates her intense interest in the world around her.

Notice the extremely large jowl and soft eye, which indicate unusual intelligence, the fine ears and the refinement of her nostrils and upper lip, which also show a clever, curious, mentally quick and extroverted nature. This is a horse whose clever mind can make her strong willed, but she is willing to cooperate if she's treated like the intelligent being that she is.

According to Leia's owner, she's been an excellent brood mare and has even adopted orphan foals. A real "matriarch," Leia is always the "boss" horse and has been known to open gates and take a whole herd down the road for an outing. Although of an independent nature, she is very trainable and competes successfully in dressage and combined driving. At the end of one event, she received a standing ovation in spite of the fact that her driver went off course, just because she is so unusually lovely to watch.

If Leia were a human, I'd say she would probably have been a movie star!

NIGHTSHADE
A six-year-old mixed breed mare, a Morgan with possibly an Appaloosa and Quarter Horse cross

When I looked at the profile of Nightshade, my intuitive reaction was one of real sadness. Oh dear, I said to myself; poor horse — unfortunate owner.

Nightshade has an enormous bulge below the eyes, a Roman head, and a small or "pig" eye; three indicators of a slow learner. Horses like this are usually completely misunderstood and misread. They are generally perceived as being very resistant, when actually they are having trouble grasping instructions. Instead of

Nightshade

understanding such a horse as we would a child with learning disabilities, we tend to think the resistant behavior is intentional, and punish the horse for it.

From the front, Nightshade displays a broad nosebone, often a sign of inflexibility. In all the pictures that I saw of the mare, her ears appeared to be uneven and different from each other, something I'd never observed before. I don't really know what this might indicate, but it's interesting to note, nevertheless. At first I thought it might be the angle at which the photographs were taken, but apparently the photos are accurate portrayals. It's possible that her ears had been damaged by the misuse of a twitch.

In addition, something about Nightshade's eyes made me wonder if she might be experiencing blurred or veiled vision; something in her "clouded" look that made me think that Nightshade might like to connect with the photographer, but that poor vision made her mistrustful. This impression was more an intuitive feeling than an actual observation. If the profile shot had showed something different, my feeling might have been wrong, but actually, the profile did support my first impression. So you see, if working from photographs, you really must have both front and side views or you can be fooled.

The story of Nightshade is a sad one. She was eventually sold at auction and probably put down, which may have been better for her, considering her tremendous difficulties. Her owner described her as hostile, aggressive and dominant, a horse who while ridden, kicked other horses in a group, was aggressive in the pasture and would constantly test the rider.

This was truly a case of mismatched horse and rider, because she was bought as a Pony Club horse and was not only too much for her child rider to handle, but was actually dangerous. Not many people have the interest, skill and time to work with what I considered to be a mentally disabled horse with a severe learning disability. In my heart I feel she's better off in "horse heaven."

Ohlone

OHLONE
A 10-year-old pony, ³/₄ Shetland and ¹/₄ Quarter Horse gelding

My first thought on seeing the photos of this pony was "what a very smart horse, what an unusual little character." Look at how wide apart his ears are, both in their setting and in the space between them at the top. Notice too, that his nostrils are large, open, and very round at the top. This small horse is wide awake! Note how the angle of the nostril from the side runs more perpendicular to the mouth line than parallel — something I've rarely seen and can only define as unusual. This characteristic may have no meaning, and may simply demonstrate how unique he is. With this combination of ear and nostril features, I would read his intelligence as being far higher than average. Ohlone, it appears to me, is a horse who thinks a great deal.

Taking the side view, note his almond eye. This type of eye often indicates an inner softness that makes for a horse who is not only gentle and cooperative, but unique in character. For practice, compare this head with those of Blaze and Winner.

Everything about Ohlone points to a strongly individual mind. He has the extremely unusual mark of five swirls on his face and, as if that's not distinctive enough, the two swirls that are side by side are fairly standard, but the one at the upper right is quite long, a good inch and a half.

In a stallion, even a triple swirl usually means unpredictability, but since Ohlone is a gelding, his multiple swirl pattern, taken together with all the other characteristics, speaks of a fascinating personality with a range of responses to everything around him well beyond the normal. (His owner says he's more human than horse!)

It's especially important to treat a highly complex animal like this with respect, and to recognize him as an individual and not just a pony. Many people

five weeks old

Savannah Wind

have a tendency to push ponies around because they're small, but this little horse has so much going on in his mind that if you try to dominate him without respecting his individuality, you can be pretty sure you'll be met with resistance. If you do respect him, a horse with the special characteristics of Ohlone is a delight.

SAVANNAH WIND
An Anglo-Arab mare shown at five weeks and at two years

At five weeks you can already see what wonderful intelligence this foal has. She's bright as a silver button. Her beautiful almond-shaped eye is set low on her head, she has a lot of length from the protruding cheekbone down to the muzzle, which itself is long, and her ears are as delicate and curved as tulip petals, all indications of high intelligence.

You can see that as a two-year-old she has retained that calm and very smart look about her. Her jowl has developed more, and note the subtle dish face combined with the very slight moose nose.

The ears, with their unusual broadness through the middle, show an extremely steady and reliable character, and note, too, the strong single swirl directly between the eyes, again pointing to a highly stable individual.

Savannah Wind gives every indication of becoming a wonderful horse, beautifully balancing sensitivity, intelligence and stability. Her owner reports that she loves to learn and is very eager to please. Due to her unusual intelligence, she has her own opinions, but she is trusting, loving and cooperative. Savannah Wind is another horse of the type who must definitely be recognized and respected as an individual, or she will lose trust in humans and become resistant.

In the photo session for this book, she was confident and easy to handle, "almost as though she enjoyed posing for her portrait," says photographer Jane Reed. She is a real character, with her own mind.

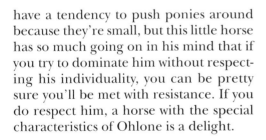

Winner

WINNER
A 17-year-old Morgan gelding

Winner's head is the perfect example of an uncomplicated, cooperative horse. From the side view: Note the straight profile denoting stability, the very square muzzle again indicating stability, the softness of the chin and the openness of the medium-sized nostrils that denote a cooperative, easy going nature. Notice the softness of the eye.

This is a very honest head — look at the front view, his willingness to look directly at us, the rather large eye, the ears that are wider apart at the top than at the base, once again indicating a compliant and cooperative nature. The long, low swirl starting from below the eyes and extending upward (must be about four inches long) is yet again another mark of a very friendly horse.

The mouth line is fairly long and full, which shows intelligence, and the upper lip is flat rather than heart shaped, indi-

cating a horse who will not test his rider. Winner will be kind, cooperative and at the same time, self-confident.

SHOMAN
A three-year-old Shagya Arabian gelding

This horse has one of the nicest characters I've ever evaluated — I'd love to have him as my companion.

In profile, note the extreme dish face in combination with the long moose nose, which shows him to possess extraordinary sensitivity and thoughtfulness, and great depth of character. Notice, too, that Shoman has a very large jowl, even though he is only a three-year-old, and his muzzle shows great refinement. He has what used to be called a "teacup nose," a nose so small it could fit into a teacup. His double chin reflects great sensitivity and capacity for thought.

Shoman's eye is a pronounced almond shape with a soft triangle above it. He is a

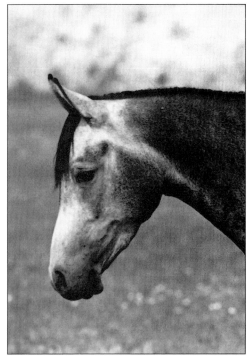

Shoman

very gentle being who needs a person who will understand him and handle him with care and consideration for his soft nature. This is a horse one would choose for pleasure and not to take over a tough course or to a polo match.

Even from the front view, you can see how Shoman's head tapers to his small nose. Observe his large eyes and the broad space between them, and notice his beautiful, fluted ears. His nostrils are narrow, an indication that this young horse is still lacking mental development. Photographs of Shoman taken two years from now would show these nostrils as at least 40 percent wider.

Shoman belongs to Jane Reed. He started out as being very willing to please, mellow and easy to train. When put on the longe line, he had no problem going forward. But under saddle he was extremely reluctant, so Jane sent him to a trainer. When she went to pick him up she was told that he was difficult out on the trail, refusing to cross a bridge that led back to

his paddock. He had crossed a similar bridge daily in Jane's pasture.

Jane wanted to see exactly what was going on, so she asked the trainer to take her and the horse to the problem bridge. When they got there Jane discovered a loose board that flipped up right in the middle of the bridge. The trainer began flapping things behind the horse, trying to chase him across it and Shoman became extremely upset. Jane calmed him, talked to him, showed him the board and then walked back and forth across the bridge with him until he was able to cross without fear, and without stepping on the board.

The moral of this story is that it is usually unwise to send this type of overly sensitive, dish-faced, gentle being out for training. The person raising this type of horse is much better off starting him with slow methods that allow the horse to understand what it is that is being asked of him.

Wizard

WIZARD
A 20-year-old Arabian gelding

Wizard is 7/8ths Arabian. He is a legend in the world of endurance riding, the winner of 25 endurance competitions, five of them 100 miles, the rest 50. Wizard's pulse and respiration recovery are amazing — he has won 18 "Best Condition" awards.

This horse has a noble and elegant Arabian head that's just about as intelligent as you can find. First of all, look at his profile; he has a very long nose from the protruding cheekbone down to the upper lip, and he also has a slight moose nose. These two characteristics together show him to be both very stable and highly intelligent.

Unusual intelligence is evidenced again in the long, flat, narrow chin and the narrow space between the mouth and chin. Horses with these characteristics are very fast learners.

The lips and nostrils are unusually expressive and mobile. Note that the nostrils are quite large and long in proportion to the rest of the head. The ears are delicate and refined, even though they are set a shade closer at the top, which usually means a hot temperament, and the jowl is large, all signs of a very active mind and a developed intellect. Wizard gives the impression of being so intelligent that he would be able to control himself in spite of those "hot" ears.

Karen Kroon, his owner and a top endurance rider, says that she can ride Wizard across treacherous ground at all speeds and still feel perfectly safe. "He rarely takes a wrong step," she says, "and when he does, he carefully picks up his foot and puts it down safely somewhere else."

Karen has also fox hunted Wizard, using him as a gate horse because he stands so quietly while 30 or more other horses go flying by. Wizard is a wonderful teaching horse, who works especially well with children who are learning to ride.

Tubbs

TUBBS
A 14-year-old Quarter Horse gelding

Evaluating this horse's head was great fun for me. My first impression, on looking at the side view, was of a horse who just exudes pride, self assurance, inner strength and determination and is most likely set in his ways. These qualities are reflected by the self-assured look in the eye, the complex chin with a point, which can become hard when he's determined to do what he wants, and the prominent nosebone below the eye, which further expresses determination and, at times, a tendency toward inflexibility. His attitude seems to say, "I know what I'm doing, I know what I want, and maybe you can fit into the picture."

Tubbs has a long mouth. He has a great deal of unusual definition around the muzzle, which slopes down across the nostrils, has a little dip and then a flat plane to the mouth, denoting determination and intelligence. Note, too, the flatish chin with the small lump on it, again a signal to us that Tubbs is a smart horse.

From the front, we see that Tubbs has a large, curious eye, quite a bit of breadth between the eyes, very refined nostrils although they are a little on the small side, and lips that are fine, showing intelligence. The flexibility of the upper lip indicates curiosity. His ears are short, and on this long head I'd say they are close to being pin ears, indicative of horses who are very determined and often considered stubborn.

Tubbs has a tendency to buck at the canter. His owner tells me he demands respect, is smart and strong, as well as willful if you get on his wrong side. If he likes you, Tubbs gives you no trouble at all.

This is the kind of horse who needs a very special rider, one who respects a horse for his intelligence but who also demands respect from the horse in return. To get along with Tubbs, a rider must show equal strength of mind and character.

Tulip

TULIP
A two-year-old Quarter Horse mare

Looking at the side view, the first thing that jumped out at me about this filly's head was a sense of both alertness and sweetness. Tulip's jowl has not yet reached mature development, so the head may seem a little long and narrow, but she does display a combination of features which indicate high intelligence: The look of curiosity, interest and softness in her eye, the strongly defined upper lip which protrudes just a little bit, and the softly pointed chin.

She has just the slightest concave sweep to her nose, not enough to identify as a dish face, but just enough to add the characteristic of sensitivity to the mixture of traits in her personality.

From the front view, the first thing that struck me was her incredibly wide-set, broad, short and almost lopped ears, indicating stability, a horse that will be a consistent and willing performer.

Notice, too, Tulip's two swirls side by side in the middle of her head above the eyes. When I consider this double swirl in relation to the rest of her characteristics, I believe that she will not be prone to unexpected bursts of emotion that these swirls can indicate.

Tulip's nostrils are narrow and undefined as yet, which is quite common in a two-year-old, since it indicates lack of mental development. She's a little narrow over-all in the head, which can indicate a horse who will do what you ask, if you are clear with your aids, instead of having her own ideas about what to do. This willingness and interest in what you wish her to do are further indicated by her soft, heart-shaped upper lip.

Tulip's owners confirm my observation, describing her as both smart and kind, a horse who never bucked or offered any resistance when they were starting her under saddle; it took her only two days to learn to longe at the walk, trot and canter.

Tez

TEZ
A 12-year-old half-Quarter Horse, half-Arab gelding

My first "take," on looking at Tez's profile, was the impression of a sharp and hot personality. It was an intuitive feeling, and I just couldn't quite get to the root of what was inspiring it. After gazing at the photograph for a while, I realized that Tez has unusual ears; they are angled steeply forward, giving them an appearance of "sharpness." There is also a look of determination in his eye that attracted me, and I had the sense of a quiet, strong will. For some reason, however, I was finding him very difficult to analyze.

The reading became easier when I turned for guidance to the front view. Here, I saw very large nostrils and large eyes (notice how much of the eye shows), both indications of intelligence, and very short, broad ears, with a steep forward slope as seen from the side, often signaling a horse who is hot and complicated.

If his ears had combined length and broadness, they would have indicated stability, but here, the shortness of the ear points to a tendency for the horse to be set in his ways and the sharp forward angle intensifies this tendency. However, the look in his eye and the softness around his muzzle indicates a basically sweet nature, as does the profile, which suggests to me a personality that is hot and complex, but also kind.

Tez has a fascinating history. He was on his way to the "killers" and was for sale for $400 when his owner rescued him. Up to that point, he had never been able to be ridden without being tranquilized. Apparently, even while out of shape and on tranquilizers, he had been able to go up any mountain at a trot without tiring. His owner tells me that his energy is amazing; there is no "quit" about him. When coming home, he jigs the whole way, and nothing can deter him. This would certainly accord with the forward set of his ears. On the one hand, he has an incredible will

Yuma

and stamina, but on the other, he's very sensible, doesn't shy, loves to work and is very friendly.

My final impression of Tez is that he is unusually intelligent, and if he could talk he'd have a lot to say.

YUMA
A five-year-old mustang gelding

The Federal Bureau of Land Management conducts periodic round-ups of wild mustangs to control the population of the herds. Part of the Bureau's program is an adopt-a-horse plan, which is how Joanne and Jim Dietz of Santa Cruz, California, came to own Yuma.

After his adoption, Yuma went to a mustang trainer in Idaho; when he came home he was covered with rope burns, because, the trainer said, he had been "extremely stubborn and difficult to break."

This is a horse who looks very different when you compare the front with the side

view, another good example of why it's important to look at both views in order to come to a correct evaluation.

From the front, his large, expressive, nostrils should indicate intelligence, but his small eye set high on the head suggests a horse who could have streaks of inflexibility, one who would need to take a little time to figure things out. It's possible that the nostrils are more developed because he does not see clearly.

Yuma's ears are very interesting. From the front view you can see that they are set fairly wide apart, but they are narrow and stand straight up, another sign of inflexibility and slow thinking.

When I say "inflexible," I speculate that horses like Yuma actually have fewer neural signals coming from the brain than do other horses. I get the impression that with this type of horse there isn't as much connection from the brain to the body as there is with a horse who is a fast learner. This means there may be a physiological reason for what is sometimes viewed as a "bad attitude."

There is a gentle but reserved look in the horse's eyes, an introverted expression.

The swirl is very long — you can see it starts about two inches below the eye and extends up above the eye — a good, four-inch-long swirl. In our studies and in my experience, we've repeatedly seen this type of swirl on horses who have a really friendly nature. So basically, if you are patient, this is a horse with whom you can develop a relationship of trust and friendliness even though he is difficult. His large nostrils, softness of chin line and squareness of muzzle indicate that he is capable of being cooperative provided you allow him enough time to figure out what it is you're asking of him.

Going on to the side view, we can see a Roman nose and an extreme bulge on the frontal bone below the eye, and a short mouth. This signals a character who may be tough and bold but also very inflexible when pushed, so it's not surprising to me to hear that he fought his trainer. Some-times, when the mouth is short, it is difficult for the horse to carry a bit easily, so there can be a good deal of resistance. The mouth also has a strong connection to the limbic system, the part of the brain that affects emotions and learning ability. Therefore, if there are problems concerning the mouth, it can affect a horse's capacity for cooperation and learning.

If you use even the standard methods to break such a horse or, worse, if you try to fight him, he will have a tendency to hurt himself rather than give in, because he really can't help his resistance. It is not intentional.

My overall impression of Yuma is that he's not a horse you prevail over and "tame": He's a horse you have to teach with a great deal of patience and consideration for his mental shortcomings. He's a horse for a person who is a real character too, someone who would appreciate his wildness, his independence and that little bit of distance and reserve that he would maintain until he could develop enough trust to give you his heart.

PART TWO

HEALTH:
ITS EFFECT ON PERSONALITY

CHAPTER FIVE

Conformation

How does conformation affect character and behavior? The basic proportions of a horse determine balance, movement and athletic ability; physical balance affects emotional and mental balance. If a horse is splay-footed, ewe-necked, "coon-footed," long-backed, or base-narrow, or if the angles of the shoulder, pastern and hoof do not align, his athletic ability and self-confidence will usually be limited.

It's valuable to be able to recognize ideal conformation as well as conformation faults which may inhibit a horse's performance. If a rider can evaluate a horse's potential from his conformation, many resistances and fights can be avoided, resistances that are created when a horse is asked to perform in a way that is impossible and results in an incorrect character analysis.

The following descriptions, drawings and case studies will help you to understand the relationship between conformation and personality.

Conformation Measurements and Proportions

Ideal conformation:

These measurements will give you a way of checking for ideal conformation for an athletic horse. The head, neck, shoulders, back and croup will be the same length in ideal Thoroughbred conformation. The shoulder is measured from the point of the shoulder to the middle of the withers. The back is measured from the middle of the barrel (behind the scapula) to the flank. The head is measured from the top of the poll to the upper lip at the edge of the mouth. The croup is measured from the point of the hip over the point of the buttock to the center line under the tail. Other breeds vary and in hundreds of horses I've measured, the croup may be up to four inches shorter than the other measurements. However, this doesn't seem to affect athletic ability in the least.

The neck is measured from behind the ear to the front of the scapula when the neck is level, not raised. If the horse is just a pleasure horse the length of the neck is not so important. However, if you are asking for exceptional athletic ability or collection, the neck should be the same length as the shoulders, head, and back (fig. 1).

The angle from the center of the fet-

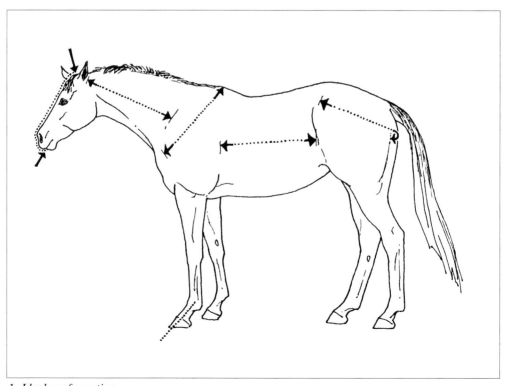

1. Ideal conformation

lock joint down through the center of the pastern and through the hoof, should match the angle of the shoulder. When the shoulder and pastern angles don't match, stiffness and pain can be the result, causing unwillingness, unsoundness and resistance.

Long back:

Measuring the length from behind the scapula to the flank you'll sometimes find in a long-backed horse that the back is about four inches longer than the head, neck or shoulder (fig. 2).

How does the long back affect personality? Doreena pictured on page 103 is a good example of a long-backed, loose-coupled, stick-necked and ewe-necked horse. A long back can result in pain and problems in responding satisfactorily to a rider's demands, with the result that the horse's behavior may be mistaken as evidence of "bad character."

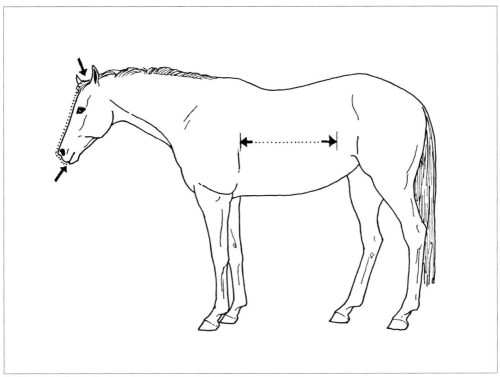

2. Long back

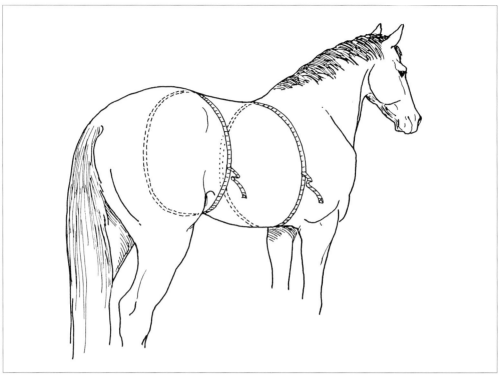

3. Measuring girth and flank

Measuring the girth and the flank:

In 2500 B.C. *The Art of Horsemanship* was written by the Greek general, Xenophon. In this treatise he states that a well-balanced horse can be measured by laying one's open hands on both sides of the loin area. The loins should be so broad that the hands can lie flat on either side of the spine. Remember, in Xenophon's time horses were ridden bareback and appeared to be quite short backed. However, his principle is worth bearing in mind.

The Hungarian cavalry horses of the past were famous for their endurance, and the best of these were said to measure an equal circumference around the flank area as that around the heart girth. I have measured many 100-mile endurance horses to test this theory and have found that it often holds true. For instance, my Arabian mare, Bint Gulida, who set a record in 1961 for a hundred miles in 13 hours 36 minutes, winning first place and the Best Condition trophy, had these measurements.

It is easy to measure your horse's heart girth and flank. You will need a length of rope or a tape measure that will not stretch. To measure the heart girth, place the rope over the middle of the withers so it lays slightly behind the elbows, making sure it falls perpendicular to the ground on both sides of the horse. Then measure the heart girth circumference. To measure the flank, place the rope across the loins so it falls perpendicular to the ground along the fullest part of the flank, just in front of the stifle. Check to be sure the rope is even on both sides of the horse. Then measure the flank circumference. The average horse measures approximately one to two inches less around the flanks than around the heart girth (fig. 3).

4. Herring gut

Herring gut:

The measurement around the flank of a herring-gutted horse can be as much as four inches (or more) less than the heart girth measurement. It's difficult to keep a saddle on a herring-gutted horse with-out a snug breast plate and a very tight girth. Either of these can irritate a horse resulting in resistant or erratic behavior (fig. 4).

Normal and Abnormal Conformation

Front Legs/Front View

Normal:

To check correctness of conformation, which ultimately affects not only physical but often mental and emotional balance, drop a plumb line from the chest down the front leg. This should then pass the middle of the forearm, the middle of the knee, the middle of the fetlock joint and the middle of the hoof (fig. 5).

Base wide:

Base-wide, broad-chested horses tend to be on the slow side, whereas base-wide, narrow-chested horses can have poor balance and as a result may be skittish. See the Arabian gelding Kesil, pictured on page 106, for a good example of an unbalanced, base-wide, narrow-chested horse (fig. 6).

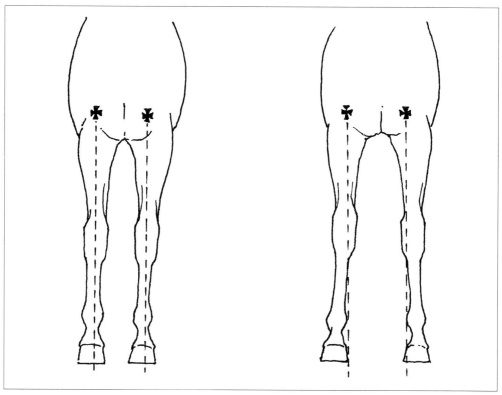

5. *Normal*   6. *Base wide*

Base narrow, toes out, narrow chest, slant knees:
Limited weight-carrying ability; frequently lack self-confidence and are fearful, flighty, unreliable and poor athletes, due to the mental and emotional imbalance that accompanies physical imbalance. May be accompanied by a high head carriage or a ewe neck (fig. 7).

Pigeon toes:
Though their athletic ability is sometimes limited, these horses are usually stable and can make great pleasure mounts (fig. 8).

Base wide, toes out:
This conformation defect rarely affects personality, but does usually limit athletic performance (fig. 9).

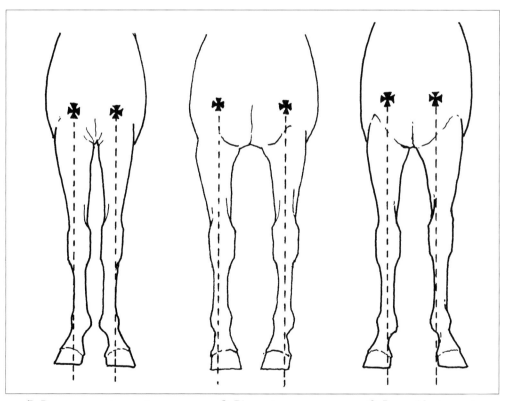

7. Base narrow, toes out   8. Pigeon toes   9. Base wide, toes out

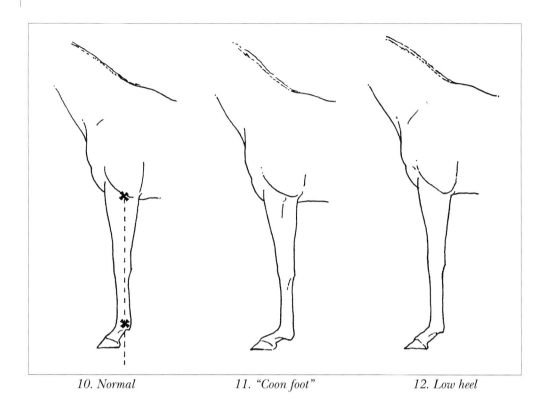

10. Normal   11. "Coon foot"   12. Low heel

Front Legs/Side View

Normal:
For ideal soundness and balance a plumb line should pass through the center of the forearm, center of the knee and center of the fetlock joint (fig. 10).

"Coon foot" and low heel:
Both of these conformation faults can lead to soreness and back pain, resulting in resistance and limited performance (figs. 11 & 12).

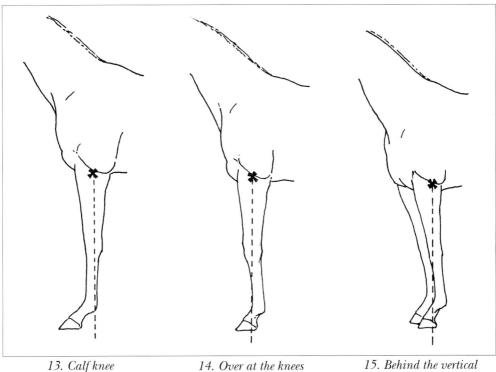

13. Calf knee   14. Over at the knees   15. Behind the vertical

Calf knee:

For light work on the flat, this fault may not be a problem. For jumping and fast work, strain and limited ability may cause horse to have problems (fig. 13).

Over at the knees:

Tension in the legs, shoulders and back can result from this fault, often causing flightiness or nervous behavior. On the other hand, several of the top steeple-chasers I've known have been over at the knees (fig. 14).

Behind the vertical:

This physical imbalance is a common cause of nervousness or resistance (see Doreena, page 103). Many horses can be helped with TTEAM work on their bodies (fig. 15).

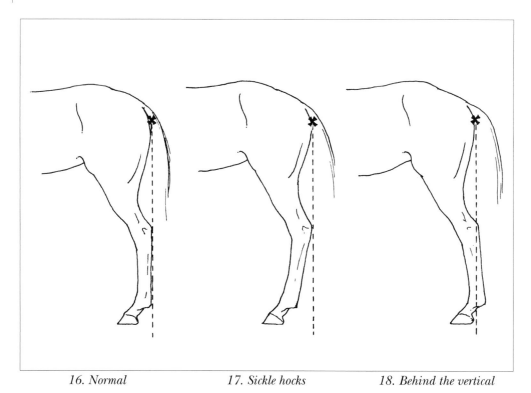

| 16. Normal | 17. Sickle hocks | 18. Behind the vertical |

Hind Legs/Side View

Normal:
Balanced; the plumb line drops from the point of the buttocks, passes along the back of the hock and the back of the fetlock joint (fig. 16).

Sickle hocks:
With overwork, the sickle-hocked horse may develop curbs, muscle knots or tightness in the gaskin, which frequently cause resistance (fig. 17).

Behind the vertical:
The conformation fault that most affects the personality will be found in horses who stand behind the vertical. These horses are usually difficult to collect and will often show resistance at higher levels of athletic endeavor. Such resistance, usually interpreted as intentional stubbornness or unwillingness, can actually be the result of back pain, pelvic pain and inability to perform (fig. 18).

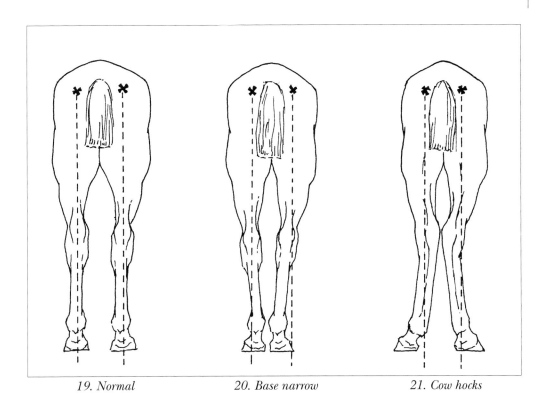

19. Normal   20. Base narrow   21. Cow hocks

Hind Legs/Rear View

Normal:
A plumb line drops from the point of the buttocks through the point of the hock, fetlock joint and heel (fig. 19).

Base narrow:
Although I've seen top jumpers with this conformation, this fault can cause lack of self-confidence and nervousness from strain on the pelvis and back due to compensation for imbalance (fig. 20).

Cow hocks:
Extreme cow hocks can cause resistance due to weakness and fatigue when athletic demands are too difficult. When combined with loose coupling, this conformation can result in a bad attitude from soreness or lack of strength in the back, loin and hindquarters (fig. 21).

Backs

Loose coupling:

This fault needs to be watched and considered carefully when choosing a horse. I see many personality problems when horses are pushed beyond their capacity because of loose coupling. See Doreena, page 103 (fig. 22).

Sway back:

One of the greatest difficulties in cases of sway back is getting a saddle to fit so that it does not cause back pain and resultant nervous and over-reactive behavior (fig. 23).

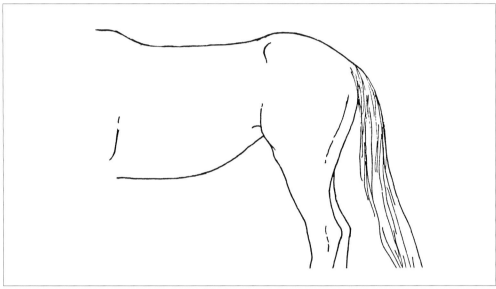

22. Loose coupling

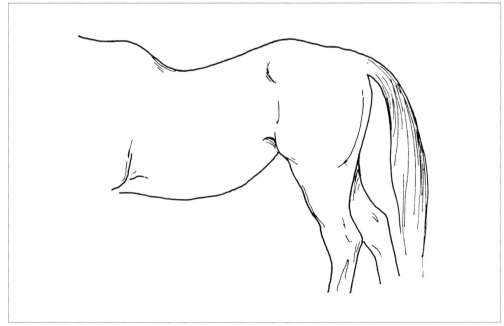

23. Sway back

Necks

Normal:

Length, thickness and set of the neck can have a major influence on behavior. A horse who has a clean throat latch and sufficient length of neck placed well on the shoulders will have natural balance and coordination (fig. 24).

"Stick neck":

Often the "stick-necked" horse can't attain the levels of collection and balance we may require. If you begin to get resistance with collected movements or performance, examine your horse's neck to see if your expectation is reasonable and physically possible (fig. 25).

Short neck with thick throat latch:

These horses often have more resistance to collection than those with "stick necks." They can make great trail horses, but if they have behavior problems, be aware of their physical limitations before you start blaming their personality (fig. 26).

24. Normal

25. "Stick neck"

26. Short neck with thick throat latch

Necks *(cont.)*

Ewe neck:

Ewe-necked horses often have difficult and resistant personalities. This is because the conformation defect causes the horse's back to drop and tighten so his breathing and balance may be affected. With TTEAM work it's possible to correct a ewe neck by bringing the back up and shifting the center of gravity. Through these changes you can dramatically aid the innate difficulties of the ewe-necked horse (fig. 27).

27. Ewe neck

High withers:

High withers are rarely a problem unless the saddle is a bad fit. Unfortunately it is difficult to get a saddle to fit a high-withered horse, so many people make do with a saddle that pinches the horse's withers and experience all sorts of behavior problems such as nervousness, bucking or bolting (fig. 28).

28. High withers

Five Illustrated Case Studies of Poor Conformation

DOREENA

This mare is a good example of a long-backed, loose-coupled, "stick-necked" and ewe-necked horse whose conformation causes pain. Bought as a dressage horse, when asked to collect into the correct frame, she gave a very unsatisfactory response to the rider's demands and was, consequently, labeled uncooperative and difficult. She was eventually sold as a western pleasure horse.

In this category, she excelled, turning from a problematic mare to a cooperative horse who made her rider happy. Because she did so well in western pleasure it was assumed she could become a reining horse, but again her conformation let her down. She had great difficulty in getting her hind legs under her on the slides, due to the imbalance caused by her long back and loose coupling. The result: major fights with her trainer and a reputation for "stubbornness." (See photo 1.)

1. Doreena's problems are caused by a long back, loose coupling, and a stick neck that is also ewed.

WAGNER

A 10-year-old Quarter Horse, Wagner has been known to blow up and buck at least once in the majority of his training sessions and was considered "a real jerk" by his trainer. Examine the photographs of him closely and you may be able to see the cause of much of his problem. Notice the "stick neck" with a slight ewe, and the look of discomfort that he displays in all of the photos in which he is under saddle.

Wagner is another case in which a so-called "bad personality" is directly caused by poor conformation. The question here is also one of suitability for the discipline: Wagner might be fine as a field hunter, but the collected frame expected in dressage is difficult for his conformation. (See photos 2–5.)

2. Wagner: Notice the "stick neck" and slight ewe.

3. The horse's neck is very tight and he looks as though he's in pain. Observe the tenseness around the nostrils and the eye — he appears to be holding his breath, which is a common cause for a horse's blowing up and bucking.

4. Here, Wagner is significantly behind the vertical. This position is often comfortable for the rider because the horse's back gets softer, but can be very frustrating for the horse because he can't see where he's going, and pain can result from over-tight muscles in the neck and back.

5. Look at the ridge of muscle along the top of Wagner's neck. Even though he's not quite on the vertical you can see that the neck is still ewed. This tight, "stick neck" is shortened and ewed, making him resistant and inhibiting his ability to cooperate.

KESIL

Kesil, a five-year-old Arabian gelding, is a great example of a horse who is base wide, narrow chested, and toes out both in front and behind. Kesil is a very nice horse on the ground, but as soon as a rider gets on his back he becomes highly unpredictable. The gelding is a very slow learner who does not retain information, a horse who is a perfect demonstration of how physical, mental and emotional imbalance can interact to affect personality.

Kesil is not a mean horse, but his explosive reactions could certainly cause him to be labeled as such. (See photos 6–8.)

6. Kesil: A five-year-old Arabian gelding who is base wide, narrow-chested and toes out both in front and behind.

7. A typical reaction for Kesil. In spite of the fact that the horse has been ridden many times, he still tosses his head and tightens his tail in fear when the rider puts her leg over the saddle.

8. A first glance gives the impression of a rather sweet personality. Note however, the thin, "stick neck" which is slightly ewed and the high head carriage which is apparently typical of this horse. There is a lack of maturity in the look about the head — in spite of the fact that he is a five-year-old, his jowl is very small, and he has a rather dreamy expression in his eye.

CHOCOLATE:

When I first looked at the photos of the head of this 13-year-old pony gelding named Chocolate, I thought, hmmmm, dependable. There's something really nice about him with his straight profile, broadly spaced eyes, ears and large nostrils. However, when I looked at the profile once more, it became apparent to me that the head was set on the neck in a rather tight way, a sight that set off an intuitive warning in me. After you've become practiced at evaluations, you'll find that your intuition will develop, like an inaudible inner voice. In this case, my intuition told me, "uh-oh, this pony is over-alert."

In this situation, I needed to look at the whole body to get the full picture. The body shows Chocolate to be high-headed, ewe-necked, long-backed and tight in the muscles of his hindquarters and rump — he's wound up like a coiled spring and that's the way he moves under saddle.

Chocolate's owner reports that though he's under 13 hands, he always has to be the first one in the pack. He isn't dangerous, she says, but she goes on to describe him as "a real, little fireball."

I believe his nervousness and his restive personality are caused not by his mental or emotional qualities but by his conformation—a case of the body ruling the mind. (See photos 9–11.)

9. Chocolate: Notice his broad ears, large nostrils, and eyes spaced wide apart, all of which taken together denote an intelligent, dependable nature.

10. Despite the straight profile indicating an uncomplicated and easy-going nature, note the tension in the way the head is set on the neck, a clue to his nervousness under saddle.

11. Note Chocolate's conformation: High-headed, ewe-necked, long-backed and tight in the muscles of the rump and hindquarters.

12. Fjodor is high-headed by nature, which makes it uncomfortable for him to canter in a round, collected frame.

FJODOR

Fjodor is a six-year-old Akhal-Teke stallion who has a lovely disposition on the ground. He's kind, calm and easy to train, yet he can display a stubborn streak. (I've owned a number of young stallions who at certain points in their training planted all four feet on the ground and refused to move. Rather than getting into a fight, I've discovered the best thing to do is be patient and wait a few minutes.)

Fjodor was sold because he was so difficult to train at the canter. His trot was beautiful and ground-covering, but according to his rider, he was "very resistant, unconnected and high-headed" at a canter. "It felt as though his hind legs were out behind him all the time," she said.

Here we have another example of how conformation affects performance. Fjodor was expected to canter in a round, collected frame, and yet he is high headed by nature, as you can see both from the side and the front views. His front legs are set behind the vertical and his hind legs are set slightly out behind him.

If you try to force a horse like this into an uncomfortable collected frame, he may lose his innate kindness and become stubborn, resistant and antagonistic. Akhal-Tekes originate in the steppes of Asia, where they are usually ridden with a free, high head. If Fjodor had been allowed to canter in this way, he would have been able to balance himself in accordance with his build. (See photos 12 & 13.)

13. Notice how Fjodor's front legs are set behind the vertical and his hind legs slightly out behind him.

It's fascinating to see how, in horses just as in humans, self-image and self-confidence are strongly affected by the way individuals perceive and sense their bodies. When a horse has poor conformation, or certain ways of habitually holding his body, his unbalanced posture can trigger nervousness and a weak self-image.

I've been astonished to discover that, by changing this imbalanced posture through patient work with the horse, you can often see fearfulness shift to confidence. What had seemed a problem of personality simply disappears.

Work with the Tail to Create Self-Confidence

I've often noticed that when horses are fearful or lack self-confidence, they hold their tails in a set that is tight, stiff, and sometimes clamped or close to the body. In the herd situation, a horse who is holding his tail tightly is usually lacking in self-confidence and low in the pecking order of the herd. Such a horse could easily be dismissed as having a timid personality, but surprisingly, this diffidence is not necessarily a permanent characteristic. Amazingly, you can shift the attitude by working on the tail, by changing the way the horse holds the tail in relation to the body.

I've seen many cases where tail work was successful in enhancing self-confidence, but my favorite example is that of Ibn Sharaf, a beautifully bred, rose-gray, two-year-old Arabian stallion at Hof Schimmelberg (which, by the way, translates as "the court of white horse mountain") in Germany.

Ibn Sharaf was bred to stand at stud by Heinz Maltz, a successful Arabian horse breeder who lives in Munich. Heinz had asked me to come and have a look at the young stallion because he was worried. He was low in the pecking order of the herd and wasn't demonstrating the fire, presence and self-confidence necessary for a breeding stallion.

My first impression of Ibn was his tight tail held close to the body, not the elegant, high tail carriage typical of a young Arabian. I asked Heinz to catch the horse and hold him while I worked on him. The colt stood quietly while I took his tail and manipulated it vertebra by vertebra. Standing to the side of his hindquarter, I held the tail arched in both my hands, circling it first in one direction and then another, then pulling from behind and slowly releasing (page 166). The whole session took about seven minutes.

When we turned Ibn Sharaf back into the herd he behaved like a different horse; his stride had more spring and he held his tail high and arched. Now the horse truly looked like an "Ibn" or son of his elegant sire, Sharaf. In addition, and to my complete surprise, over the next few months the young stallion began to advance himself in the pecking order. His whole carriage, self-image and position in the herd had shifted. He had gained his self-confidence.

Examine the Feet

There are other aspects of conformation that can affect personality. They are the angles of the shoulder, pastern and hoof. When the angle from the withers to the point of the shoulder does not match that of the angle through the center of the pastern and the hoof (fig. 1, page 90), pain can occur in the back, shoulders, legs and hooves. It's important, therefore, when evaluating your horse's personality, to examine these angles. They may give you a clue to behavior that does not correspond to the characteristics of your horse's head.

I've seen some Arabians and Thoroughbreds with this condition whose reaction is to become very nervous, irritable and uncooperative. Quarter Horses, on the other hand, have the opposite response. They become resigned to the pain and tend to slow down. As a result they are often mistakenly labeled as having lazy personalities. In all cases the horses are acting different from normal because of soreness all through their bodies caused by poor feet.

It's important, therefore, when evaluating your horse's personality, to make sure to look at his feet. They might give you the answer to what may otherwise seem inexplicable behavior.

There are many good books written on the subject of ideal angles for the hoof. I believe it's worthwhile cultivating a knowledge of the subject. One book you might enjoy is Tony Gonzales' *Proper Balance Movement.*

CHAPTER SIX

Soreness and Pain

In 1982, I went to Wurtzberg, a beautiful German town nestled beside the river Main, to teach my TTEAM method of training and riding. While I was there, I met a charming veterinarian who invited me to have dinner with her family. Of course we wound up discussing my TTEAM training methods with her husband, also a veterinarian. My interest was particularly caught by his description of a Polish horse he was treating for lameness, who had what he termed a very difficult personality.

"Just the horse for you to work on, Linda," he said with a skeptical smile. "The horse won't allow anyone in the stall with him. He's so aggressive you have to watch him every minute. As soon as you turn your back on him, even for a second, he'll bite you."

The next day I went to visit the horse. I stood outside his stall and looked him over, and he looked me over. His head was long and narrow, indicating a horse who is willing, provided you give clear commands. His ears were narrow and not very well defined, indicating a nature that could be somewhat changeable. His nostrils, too, were narrow, signifying mental slowness. However, the expression in this horse's eye was reasonable. To me, he didn't have the hot personality profile that I would have associated with a horse who was overly aggressive or dangerous.

When I asked my friend's permission to go into the stall with the horse, he shook his head and said the German equivalent of "be my guest."

I went in calmly, keeping my mind clear of preconceptions, because when most animals sense fear or apprehension they very naturally mirror it right back to you. Instead, I projected an attitude of, "What can be wrong with you? Would you permit me to check your body?" It seemed to work. Although he was tense and irritable at first, the horse quieted enough to allow me to examine him, and I was surprised to find that not only was he lame, he was also extremely sensitive to my lightest probe, and sore over all his body.

Looking at his conformation, I could understand why he was having such a problem with pain; his pasterns were short and straight, he had a very straight shoulder and the angle of the shoulder and the pastern was different, making it difficult for him to carry a rider's weight.

After examining him I worked his entire body with the TTouch, and it was wonderful to see how his whole attitude changed. After an hour-long session he began to relax and stopped trying to kick and bite. Here was a horse whose aggressive actions came not from personality defect but from the pain. The veterinarian was surprised. The connection between pain and this type of aggressive behavior was a new concept for him.

Pain in the horse's body and the attendant fear expressed as aggression, resistance or other reflexive responses, can often be the result of the exercises we demand of horses. Sometimes the style of riding, or the particular sport — jumping, dressage, endurance, cutting, driving or whatever — and its particular demands, are not appropriate for the body type of the horse, putting too much mental and/or physical stress on the animal. Other times a horse can develop muscle strain or soreness from overwork, from not warming up sufficiently before collected work, or from being ridden in an over-collected frame without being allowed to lower the head and stretch out the neck.

This stretching of the neck is important. Long periods of training in an over-collected frame will cause a horse's neck muscles to lose blood circulation and elasticity. Approximately two hand widths behind the ears is an acupuncture point for blood circulation to the brain. When the neck muscles become contracted, circulation to the brain is interrupted and pain is one result. This can cause a horse to become resistant, aggressive or stubborn.

An instance of this was the case of a dressage horse named Buket, a Russian Thoroughbred I worked with at the Bitsa Sports Complex in Moscow. Bitsa Horse Center was built for the 1980 Olympic horse events and later became the center where horses and riders are trained for national and international dressage, jumping and three-day eventing competitions. It is an extensive place, with two arenas, one for warm-up and the other a huge show hippodrome with seats for 2,000 people and a 15-foot stained glass window at the one end.

I had come to Moscow at the invitation of Dr. Nina Kanzina, Bitsa's chief veterinarian, to work with the Olympic teams. We had a hilarious time, dictionaries in hand, trying to overcome the language barrier. Of course, once we started working hands on with the horses, we were speaking an international language.

Buket, a bay gelding ridden by Olympic rider Uri Koushov, had been successful and cooperative until, without apparent cause, he became a different horse, bucking under the rider every time he was asked to execute a flying change. Buket had a lovely, intelligent head, with no quirk bumps — nothing that would suggest a resistant or unreliable nature.

Extensive veterinary examination failed to find a physical explanation for his explosive behavior. Since the veterinarians could find nothing physically wrong and diagnosed his behavior as resistant, Buket's rider, following conventional wisdom, had punished him with whip and spur — to no avail.

When I explored Buket's body for areas of tension or soreness, I found a spot under the cantle of the saddle on the left side. In checking the range of movement of Buket's legs, I found I could not move his left hind leg in a circle of more than four inches, and his right hind leg was much stiffer than it should have been.

When I observed the horse under saddle, I saw that he exhibited pain and stress even at the walk. In the first five minutes after being mounted, he was in a white, lathered sweat with an 80 bpm (breaths per minute) respiration. (Normal respiration at the walk is under 30 bpm.) Even on a loose rein, Buket carried himself behind the vertical, the result of too much collected work without any opportunity to stretch out between exercises.

When I considered all these points together, they added up as an explanation of Buket's resistant behavior. To help correct the problem, I worked on the horse together with Copper Love, a friend and practitioner of TTEAM, who assisted me in Moscow. For three weeks I rode Buket, using a variety of exercises under saddle and from the ground, to soften his tight muscles. Twice daily, Copper worked his body with TTouches. Uri continued with this work, including riding Buket in a lindel (a type of hackamore). Nine months later, Uri and Buket (as though reborn) placed 11th in the world championship competition in Toronto. Buket's flying changes were excellent, and it was a special treat to see the outstanding partnership of this Russian horse and rider rewarded.

I've worked with many cases like Buket's, where riding in an over-collected frame without adequate extension has produced what people see as personality problems. Classical dressage emphasized giving the contracted muscles of the neck and back a chance to relax again. However, in my travels around the world, working with horses and riders in the higher levels of dressage, I've found that people talk about lengthening the frame, but in actuality, they often don't allow their horses full extension, denying the muscles a chance to relax and reoxygenate. The result: The horse's muscles keep on getting shorter and tighter until finally circulation and breathing are affected. The horse then turns sour, or begins to buck and becomes resistant in other ways.

Horses buck for a variety of reasons, though rarely because a horse was "born to be bad." Some years ago, I worked with a Peruvian stallion, Bravo, a young horse who had been well prepared to be saddled and mounted for the first time. An analysis of his head indicated he had a steady, reliable disposition, but each time he was mounted he would buck, sometimes the instant he was mounted, sometimes after a few steps.

Like many people, I was taught originally to regard a horse like this as a "stubborn" character who needed to be "bucked out." In my early years as an apprentice trainer, I had plenty of practice whipping this type of horse. There are several clear disadvantages to this method: First, it requires riding expertise; second, the horse will often build up even more resistance and develop a tendency to test new riders; and last but not least, this method is unnecessary and hardens the heart of the rider.

I've since realized that looking into the deeper causes of equine behavior not only affects my understanding of horses, but touches my own life as well. It's intriguing to approach each problem, whether equine or human, as an opportunity for learning. Approaching problems with such a spirit keeps my mind sharp and develops a kindness and empathy that carries over into my attitude towards humans as well as horses.

In the case of Bravo, my exploration of his body revealed that his stifles were very loose. Whenever he would begin to move forward with a rider on his back, the rider's weight would unbalance him, causing a "grinding" sensation in his loose stifles. This sudden sensation would then startle him into bucking.

Punishing him for bucking had already proven to be useless, his owner told me. I suggested that we work with the horse to get him to be aware of his stifles before he was mounted, and so to teach him to lose his fear of the grinding sensation. For one week we worked with him every day, slowly and calmly backing him up step by step, lifting and circling his hind legs and doing TTouches all over the stifle area. By the end of the week he was aware of the area in a different way, and when the day came to mount him again he was just fine. The stifles still "popped" but Bravo was no longer frightened by the feeling. He was able to carry a rider quietly and confidently.

If, on first being saddled, young horses have not been prepared for weight or pressure on the back and girth area, it's not uncommon for them to be cinchy, blow up, buck or try to lie down. Many horses are born tight or ticklish behind the elbows, and the best way to approach this problem is not by desensitizing the horse, but through gentle TTouches on the whole girth area (page 150). This "TTouching" releases tension and tightness, brings a new awareness of contact in the area as nonthreatening, and gives the horse a chance to learn how to breathe with the experience of such contact.

I don't mean to say that all equine problems are ones you can easily change. And, as I mentioned earlier in this chapter, sometimes you might find you have the wrong type of horse for your purposes.

A case in point: I was giving a clinic at the U.S. Equestrian Team (USET) headquarters in Gladstone, New Jersey. A Grand Prix level dressage rider who was attending asked me to have a look at a horse who was being very difficult when asked to perform the more advanced dressage movements. The rider wanted to know what she should do with the horse — persevere or sell the mare.

Apparently the rider believed that the horse, a 16.2 hand warmblood, had a bad attitude and was intentionally resistant, blowing up to avoid work. The answer to this behavior, she felt, was for her to apply pressure, but as it turned out, the more the mare was pressured, the more resistant she became.

When I looked at the horse's head, however, I saw no characteristics suggesting stubbornness or intractability. The mare had a classically beautiful head; square muzzle, straight profile, ears set a little wider apart at the top than at the base, and a nice big eye — all indications of a horse with a lovely personality. I wondered what was going on.

I noticed, also, that the horse had a shorter and heavier neck than is usually considered ideal for a high-level dressage prospect. And, on closer examination, I discovered that the crest of the mare's neck was as rigid and hard as a board, and very sore. The problem lay with her body type. She was a well-conformed horse with plenty of athletic ability but her neck was simply not made for the collection required at the higher levels of dressage. I suggested to her rider that she should not try to go to the very top with this mare but, in kindness, sell her to a less-experienced rider who could do lower-level dressage with her, requiring much less collection. The mare would be more comfortable and useful to someone who needed to learn from an experienced horse.

Developing unwanted heavy muscling of the neck just in front of the withers seems to be an occupational hazard for dressage horses. When this condition exists, horses often do blow up, resist or buck when asked for collected movement. The best thing to do in such a case is to stop pushing the horse and work to soften the area with heat and a variety of TTouches.

The warmblood was the type of horse who reacted to pain with the "fight" reflex by resisting when asked to do collected work. In another instance, I was called in to work with an Irish Thoroughbred whose personality responded to the same situation with "flight."

Kildare was being ridden in an over-collected dressage frame, his rider using heavy contact on a very short rein and lots of pressure with his legs and seat. The trouble was that Kildare just wasn't built to take this degree of collection and he would literally bolt, trying to flee from the pain.

Riders should remember: When a horse is in pain or holding his breath because he's being pushed too hard with the rider's legs or seat while being held with the hand, or if the rider is too demanding in other ways physically or mentally, the horse often has no recourse but to resist, at the least by tail wringing or head tossing, or at the worst by bucking or bolting off completely out of control.

CHAPTER SEVEN

Health and Environment

Have you ever heard someone who isn't feeling well say, "I'm a bit sick today, not really myself." It's a feeling we're all familiar with when our energies are low or we are coming down with influenza or a cold.

Our state of health and well-being affects our personality, and it is the same for horses. A horse is significantly affected by the quality of his food, exercise and living conditions.

Diet

Food is a complex and volatile element, because the wrong mix, or too much or too little, can distort your horse's natural responses. The size of a horse, the amount of exercise and the skill of the rider all need to be taken into consideration when deciding how much grain to feed.

While teaching at a sports club in Mexico City, I ran into an extreme example of what can happen when these elements are wrongly combined.

The horses I was working with were mainly jumpers, mostly Thoroughbreds and warmbloods. One, a gray 14.3 hand junior jumper gelding, was considered unmanageable and dangerous. His rider was an inexperienced, rather insecure 15 year old, and the horse had run away with her repeatedly. The gelding, well-mannered on the ground but volatile under saddle, was being ridden with a gag snaffle and running martingale. Even at the walk he was held so short his nose was literally six inches from his chest.

His head suggested a horse of medium learning ability with a slight "inflexibility" bump below the eyes, but he certainly did not have any characteristics that would explain his dangerous behavior and tendency to run away.

He had no soreness or sensitivity in his back which could have accounted for his pulling, so I put a lindel over the snaffle and mounted in order to evaluate the problem from the saddle. Although he didn't bolt, he was still too fast. He bucked a few times, not in an attempt to get rid of me, but more out of excess energy.

Because he settled fairly quickly after he was relieved of the discomfort caused by over-collection and a nervous rider, I began to suspect that this was a case of overfeeding of oats and not a behavior or personality problem. Sure enough, it turned out he was getting 12 quarts per day, the same grain ration as the other horses in his stable — only they were all 17-hand warmbloods. I suggested the horse's feed be cut back to one or two quarts a day, which changed this "incorrigible" horse into a suitable and safe mount for his junior rider.

In another case, inappropriate feeding wasn't the only reason causing a horse to have behavior problems. Red Fox, a 15-hand Quarter Horse gelding, was a beautiful chestnut whose normal value in those days would have been at least $1,500. However, I had the good fortune to buy him for only $350 for the school string at our Pacific Coast Equestrian Research Farm.

Why the bargain price? Because he was described to me as a runaway. Why did I buy him anyway? After evaluating his head, observing his conformation and checking his feeding program, I was sure he would be an excellent bet for us.

This was a horse with a really good head. A straight profile, large nostrils, a large jowl and well-set ears all indicated an intelligent and stable character. In addition, he was very well put together. However, I found out that the horse had been confined to a stall, turned out only one hour each day, and ridden infrequently. On top of this, he was fed four quarts of oats a day, a certain overload of energy for such an under-exercised horse.

My evaluations now complete, I took a chance on Red Fox and bought him.

As soon as the horse arrived home at the farm, we dramatically changed his diet and exercise program. On days when he wasn't being worked two to three hours a day, we turned him out to pasture.

In addition, we cut Red Fox's grain intake to two quarts a day — half oats and half rolled barley, a good source of "low octane" energy. Within one week, Red Fox had a complete change of mood. He began to be relaxed, calm and cooperative. Later, far from being the runaway I had ostensibly bought, he became one of the best school horses I ever had, winning both Western Pleasure and Hunter competitions and placing very well in dressage competitions up to the second level.

I've run into a number of horses in the past 15 years who were hot as firecrackers. In the end, it turned out that their unmanageable behavior was due to allergic reactions to grain, because as soon as grain was eliminated from their diets, they changed totally. These allergic responses can be compared to a child's sugar "high," or the reactions of people who are allergic to wheat.

Over feeding of vitamins or supplements can also cause excess energy and problem behavior. I remember a case years ago in which a horse who was on a "high energy" product was constantly bucking off his rider. The behavior stopped when he was taken off the product.

Many veterinarians are now suggesting that horses who do light work do not need a vitamin supplement, and yet I've seen dull, so-called lazy horses who benefited greatly from vitamins added to their grain.

"You are what you eat" is as true for horses as it is for humans.

Parasites

Horses who seem to be lazy may actually not have a lazy personality at all, but may be reflecting the debilitating effect of parasites. Often, because owners worm their horses on a regular basis, they dismiss parasites as a cause for laziness. However, worming four times a year does not necessarily mean that your horse is parasite free. At the Pacific Coast Research Farm we noted that some horses can look deceptively healthy, fat and sleek, even when still loaded with worms, and that such horses are also sometimes noticeably lethargic.

At two years old, the son of my never-to-be-forgotten endurance mare Bint Gulida had a very high parasite count, and this in spite of the fact that he had been wormed every three months from the time he was a foal, as was his dam. Because he was slightly pot bellied and not as energetic as he should have been, we suspected he might still have worms, so we had the veterinarian run a fecal check on him. Sure enough, he was still infested, so he was wormed intensively under the vet's supervision, taking into consideration the cycle of the larvae.

It is important to remember to have your horse checked for worms if he seems a little sluggish or poor looking — even if you worm him regularly — before you conclude that his lack of energy is evidence of a lazy character.

Exercise and Companionship

Many people don't realize that, for their well being, horses need exercise, not just under saddle but by being turned loose in a paddock or pasture with freedom to move, a friend with whom they can socialize, and shade and shelter from wind.

It's easy to forget that horses are beings with nervous systems and brains, and that, like us, they have emotional needs as well as physical ones. Horses who are kept cooped up and alone will react much as we would: Some become depressed and lethargic, while others may develop neurotic vices such as weaving, windsucking or stall walking.

If you have a single horse at home, make sure he has the companionship of another animal, be it a duck, a cat or a dog, or

Blue, a draft mare, is kept happy and healthy sharing life with her best friend, a donkey.

*This Icelandic stallion, Thunder, was stabled alone, and was very unfriendly until
he was adopted by his kitten companion. Now they spend hours playing together, and Thunder's
disposition is vastly improved.*

even something more exotic, like a llama. Another horse is ideal, but I've known horses who have become great pals with a donkey, a sheep, a goose and even with a kitten. In my grandfather's day on the race track, it was quite common for a stalled horse to have a goat as a companion. Horses are social creatures, and if they grow up alone or spend too much time on their own, their personalities definitely suffer.

Should you not have a friend for your horse, put a radio or tape player near his stall for company, but be sure to choose the music or the type of station carefully. You may find that whereas a lethargic horse may seem to enjoy lively rock 'n' roll rhythms and be energized by them, a horse with nervous energy will do best with soothing music. I think you will see the real difference companionship can make to your horse.

The Stable

Horses, like people, need the stimulation of other beings and a sense of belonging. It's much better for a horse's outlook if his stall is a home base where he can hang his head out and see what's going on, where he can see other horses or even children playing or people at work.

Horses are basically herd animals, but because of our fear that they may injure themselves or others, as well as an often limited choice of stabling options, many horses have to live where they can never use their teeth to scratch the back of a friend or stand head to tail swishing flies off each other.

If your only choice is a stable where the horses can't see outside and you also have no opportunity for turn-out, there are a number of factors that can make a big difference. For mares and geldings, make sure the horses can hang their heads out over box stall doors (whether inside or outside the barn) that are not discouragingly high. If your door is too high for the size of your horse, using a stall guard and opening the door during the day will help no end in keeping his mind and personality vibrant.

The size of a stall also matters a great deal. Many architects who don't know horses but are asked to design stables try to save space for economic reasons without considering a horse's mental, physical or emotional health. I often see stalls measuring 10 x 10, and while I think this may be fine for a horse under 15 hands, it's claustrophobic for larger horses, who can fit only by standing diagonally with their heads and tails in opposite corners. If you can, build your stall 12 x 12.

I've seen a number of successful stables in Europe where the partitioning walls are only four feet high with no separating wire partition above that height. This way the horses can interact socially. Of course you have to make sure that you stable only friends next to each other. If you have a stable with a solid wood partition and you're afraid that your horse will fight with the horse next to him, you can make an opening slit of three inches at eye level so that your horse can at least see his neighbor.

Bars or wire partitions above the wood section are far preferable to solid partitions. And in my opinion, metal sided stalls, which I've seen occasionally in the Western United States, have a definite negative effect on both behavior and personality. The sound of these partitions when bumped or kicked is strange. And being non-porous, they also hold in dampness.

Horses are affected by color vibrations, and images affect mood, so if your stable area is drab and enclosed, paint a landscape on the walls using the colors of the natural world. It'll cheer both you and your horse.

You can paint pleasant murals in a stall, but make sure to use non-toxic paint. If you don't want to go to this much trouble, painting the stable interior with a combination of cloud white, sky blue and grass green can also have a beneficial effect (on people, too).

Thyroid Imbalance

I find that a horse who has a crest that feels really hard — like a board — will often have a tendency to resist when he is asked to do any work that is not easy for him. This horse will often be called "stiff minded," but the fact is, the stiffness can actually be in the neck rather than the mind, and can be caused by a thyroid gland that is either over- or underactive.

Frequently a horse with an underactive thyroid will become fat and lethargic, and therefore be mistaken as having a lazy personality. Or then again, a hard-crested horse may show explosive, even aggressive behavior, symptoms of hyper-thyroidism (overactive thyroid).

Be aware, however, that a very hard crest may sometimes be the result of over-development of the muscles in the neck caused by over-collection, and the thyroid may be perfectly normal. If your horse resists when asked for higher levels of performance, do not assume that this resistance is intentional. Diagnosis is difficult but I recommend that you take all these factors into consideration.

If you suspect that your horse has a thyroid imbalance, have the horse checked by a veterinarian who can prescribe hormone treatment or a homeopathic remedy. Often such treatment can have very positive results. If your horse has a hard crest and is sore from over-collection, you must change your training methods, as I have discussed earlier in this book.

Hormonal Imbalance

In 1983, during a teaching seminar I was giving in Westphalia, Germany, I received a phone call from the coach of the Westphalian Junior Combined Training team. He wanted to discuss a five-year-old, 15.1 hand gray Thoroughbred mare who, on the first day of a 10-day training camp, had kicked and injured three children.

He told me the horse was very talented, but she clearly exhibited a "rotten personality," unsuitable for a child. Did I want to see her?

I certainly did. She sounded like a fascinating case for my clinic participants to observe, so I had her vanned over. I examined her body with the exploration TTouches and at the first pressure on the big muscles in her neck behind her ears, the mare jerked her head up, squealed and lashed out with a hind foot.

When I got to her shoulders, she had another violent reaction, squealing again, pinning her ears, and striking. When I very cautiously and lightly touched her in the groin area, she flung her hind quarters around, threw her tail in the air and squirted urine. Small wonder she was considered to have a rotten personality.

Over the years I had observed other mares who over-reacted to pressure on the body in exactly the same way. Sometimes such hyper-sensitivity can be caused by a hormone imbalance, and when it is, punishment, although understandable, is not only unfair, but doesn't work.

My next move was to spend about 25 minutes going over her entire body with varying degrees of what, to her, were invasive touches. These were short bursts of pressure with my four fingers held curved and in contact with each other — the curve a little like the curving grab of an eagle's talon. Of course, she felt threatened. She squealed, snapped and pinned her ears back the entire time.

When I first started, you'd have thought the mare was being tortured, but after a time she began to quiet down, and at the end of my 25 minute interval of bodywork, she had dropped her head and was accepting the touches. I could touch her all over her body without a reaction. I finished the session with 15 minutes of ground exercises through the labyrinth and over poles (page 170) to give her an opportunity to have a pleasant experience with a human, and be cooperative for a change.

The mare then went back to the training camp and a few days later I received the encouraging report that her personality and attitude had radically changed for the better. Of course, this is a dramatic case. Sometimes one session does accomplish seeming miracles, but frequently you need to follow up an initial session with more of the same work to arrive at a successful conclusion.

Although such hormonal imbalance in mares can be treated with hormone therapy, it isn't always successful. If your mare is showing symptoms such as those in the above case, she may need veterinary care, but do also try the TTouch. Over the years I've seen a substantial number of mares respond very well.

Veterinary acupuncture, homeopathy, veterinary chiropractic and Chinese herbs can also be very successful in cases of such extreme behavior. As increasing numbers of people see the benefits of holistic veterinary medicine, I think it will become more and more popular as an alternative method for the care of some equine problems.

Eyesight

Eyes, an old saying has it, are the windows of the soul. You can tell a great deal about a horse by his eye, as I have discussed at length in Chapter Three. There is one thing about the eye, however, that is invisible yet very important in evaluating equine personality. It is the quality of vision.

This is the difference between looking at the eyes to gain "insight" and looking at them to understand what I like to call "outsight." One is an expression of the horse's inner self, the other of how he physically sees the outside world — how his vision affects him.

Sometimes I give a clinic at Okamura, a serene ranch located deep in the piney, wooded mountains of New Mexico. At one of these training seminars, a horse was brought to us because he was depressed, unresponsive and uninterested in his surroundings. His owner told us that he stumbled frequently and lacked impulsion. I was teaching together with my sister, Robyn Hood, and we noticed that this horse never put his ears up, never made a friendly gesture and never seemed to look where he was going.

At first we were mystified, but after intently observing the horse, we realized that when you looked at him from the front, you could see only a small portion of his eyes, as they were set so far back in the side of his head. We concluded that because this eye set gave him so much trouble, and he had a hard time seeing where he was going, he had become introverted and dejected. This sort of innate vision problem is quite unusual. I have, however, seen other cases like his, and eyes set farther to the side of the head than average should be considered when evaluating a horse who is having problems.

Robyn has observed similar cases in Canada. "In Ontario," Robyn says, "I noticed two horses who were all right when other horses came up from behind them, but simply blew up and bolted if they were approached from head on at the trot or the canter. Both horses were being ridden in a very collected frame. When I examined them straight on, I saw that their eyes were set quite far back on either side of the head.

"I realized that the combination of the eye set and the collected frame (with the plane of the face perpendicular to the ground) probably meant that they weren't able to see very clearly. When another horse was ridden towards them head on, their vision, impaired by the vertical position of their heads, may have caused them to misjudge distance, making the oncoming horse seem to be closer than it actually was. As a result they reacted with panic and upset. Interestingly, when the same horses were allowed to assume a more relaxed posture, both of them just calmed right down."

Nervous, high strung horses are usually high-headed, and they fling their heads up as part of the fear reflex which triggers "flight." Of course, with their heads up, they see differently, so this in turn only serves to escalate their fear. Then, to make matters worse, the fear can make a horse so rigid that muscular pressure on the optic nerve can cause an additional blurring of vision. My feeling is that shying and bolting can often happen because a horse has poor depth perception or limited vision.

The rider's common response to such behavior is to punish the horse, making him more fearful and not necessarily solving the problem, but probably making it worse. Amazingly, often all it takes to change the behavior and seeming personality "defect" is to develop the horse's trust in the rider.

If you quietly bring a frightened horse's head down two things are likely to happen: The horse regains the visual security of seeing his world come together again, and the flight reflex is over-ridden. Lowering a horse's head acts like magic to calm a horse and override fear.

Sometimes, when I'm trying to understand a horse, when I'm seeking to find the place where personality and physical problems intersect, I feel like a detective sniffing around for clues. A case in point: My friend Gisella Bruggerman called me one day to discuss a horse she had in training. The four-year-old Hanovarian gelding, Gisella told me, was stubborn and unwilling when being led. As long as she was pulling on the rope, he would come forward, but when she released the pressure, expecting him to follow, he would simply stop and refuse to move forward. Gisella had reached the end of her patience.

We puzzled together for a while. One of the things Gisella told me was that the horse had spent his young years turned out in a pasture with one other horse, and suddenly I had a brainstorm. "I bet you the horse can't see well," I said. "He may need your guidance to follow you."

Sure enough, when Gisella checked with the farmer who raised the horse, he told her that the gelding had always stuck to his companion's side like a shadow. The gelding had clung to the other horse for guidance because his eyesight was so poor. His true nature was to be very gentle and cooperative, but since he had never moved around without the other horse present, he felt completely lost and unable to proceed unless he had guidance.

Understanding that poor eyesight was the underlying cause for the stubborn behavior helped Gisella to view her horse's personality in a completely new light and adapt her training method.

Is It the Horse Or Is It the Equipment?

Checking to see whether your equipment is right for your horse might seem a far cry from evaluating his personality, but sometimes an ill-fitting saddle or bridle or the wrong bit can create an extremely misleading situation.

At one of my clinics in Minneapolis I encountered an exquisite looking Arabian mare named Sahara Rose. The mare had a really pretty head that displayed many of the characteristics of a sensitive and cooperative personality, although she did have an unusually short mouth, which can signal a slow learner and tends to make it difficult for a horse to carry a bit.

From my analysis of her head, I assumed that she would have a good attitude. But her owner was exasperated with her. The horse never stood still, she said, and in two years of taking lessons on Sahara, she had never been able to get her to accept the bit. She had been told to simply resign herself to the fact that her mare was a stubborn and resistant horse, and had been advised to get rid of her.

Since I didn't "read" the horse that way, I asked the owner what the mare had been expected to do. First she had tried Western pleasure, she said, but the horse was too tense for the slow jog and low head carriage required. Then she had tried dressage but she was unable to get the mare on the bit and into a collected frame. Finally she had decided to trail ride, but Sahara jigged and made her rider miserably uncomfortable.

On examining the horse, I saw that her throat latch was thick, interfering with her ability to be collected. She had hardened, enlarged lymph nodes. Therefore, whenever Sahara had been collected as in dressage or, in a different way, in Western pleasure, she would quite naturally be very uncomfortable, tossing her head up and down repeatedly. It was this physical limitation, I pointed out, that was keeping her from cooperating. I decided to give her a free head to see how she would respond.

I rode her without a bridle, using only a neck rope, and she was absolutely wonderful. She held her head a little high, but she walked, trotted and cantered freely and no longer tossed her head. Several other people then rode her and she became the clinic favorite, much to her owner's astonishment.

I suggested to the owner that she continue to ride the mare in her natural frame as a trail horse and that, taking into consideration her short mouth, she use a lindel, the special type of bitless bridle that would probably eliminate her jigging on the trail.

Many people don't make the connection between tack and the way a horse is behaving. An incorrectly fitting saddle, for instance, can cause a number of behavioral problems. I discovered a perfect example of this while I was in Israel in 1979, traveling close to the Jordanian border among sandy hills dotted with the green oases of irrigated orchards and fields. I visited a stable where my eye was caught by a 14.3 hand, rather pitiful looking black gelding. He was a grade type of horse that the stable used on its rent string, but there was something very touching about him. "What's his story?" I asked.

The stable manager shrugged his shoulders. "Oh, this horse is going to the killers next week," he said. "He bites and kicks and he's extremely aggressive."

To me, the horse's head type just didn't match that description at all. He had a common, undifferentiated head, and though he didn't look very smart, he certainly didn't look mean. In addition, he had one long swirl right between his eyes, usually an indication of a friendly character who would enjoy people.

"Do you mind if I just work on him and check his body out?" I asked.

We cross-tied the horse so he couldn't bite. I reached up to check his neck, and found it very hot behind the ears. When I checked his back, I discovered that he had large, inflamed sores right behind the withers.

I asked to look at his saddle, and the cause of the sores was immediately clear. The saddle did not fit him correctly, sitting directly on his high withers and digging into the hollows on each side of the withers. This little horse was simply reacting to pain with the natural reflexes of fear and aggression. Kicking and biting were the only language he had to express his discomfort.

The stable manager was not unique in not connecting the sores on his horse's back with an ill-fitting saddle and resultant aggressive behavior. I've found that many riders — both inexperienced and very experienced — don't make these connections and often fail to recognize a problem stemming from a poor fit.

To check a saddle's fit, place your hand in the gullet of the saddle along the side of the withers and slide your hand down under the front of the panel and flap. If the saddle is too narrow or the panel digs into the back, you will not be able to slide your hand under without getting pinched. If you are being pinched, the horse will be, too, and the saddle is too narrow. Make sure that you conduct this check with the weight of the rider in the saddle, or your findings will not be accurate.

The stable manager was very interested in my diagnosis, and after observing me using the TTouch on the horse, he agreed to continue working on the gelding's neck and back, and to exchange the saddle for one that was more appropriate and had more padding.

Now, if this horse's head had displayed signs of a difficult character — a sunken eye, a very short mouth and very narrow nostrils, or a pronounced Roman head or a bump below the eyes, I might have moved on. But he was simply an ordinary horse with reasonable characteristics whose pain had temporarily distorted his nature.

This was one of the many times that I have been really grateful for the gift of reading equine personality.

PART THREE

BRING OUT THE BEST
IN YOUR HORSE

CHAPTER EIGHT

Matching Horse and Rider

The rare sight of a horse and rider moving together in absolute harmony and effortless beauty almost always elicits a lightening of the heart.

After that initial moment of pure delight comes our conscious judgment: We are impressed with the exquisite training of the horse and the precision of the rider; we are often aware of the many hours of work that have gone into this very effortlessness. But the key element here is one that we seldom think of — the fact that what we are witnessing is a partnership of personalities, the rapport of two separate individuals.

When buying a horse, how can you figure out if he has the potential to have a successful relationship with you? How do you know whether a horse is the best match, not only for your temperament, but for your level of experience and type of riding? How can you recognize whether difficulties between you and your horse are due to a basic personality mismatch or to a correctable misunderstanding? When should you give up and start over with another horse who will be more suitable to your needs?

Over the years and across all the thousands of cases I've analyzed, I've come to see that equine personality evaluation is precisely at its most useful when dealing with questions such as these.

Mix, Match and Mismatch

The first time I made an evaluation of a match between horse and rider was in 1978. I was teaching a training course in the Black Forest region in Germany. One of the participants was a teacher, Maria, a sensitive young woman with a lively mind and a wide range of interests. She loved the idea of riding out into the forest with an equine companion who would be curious about the world around him and who would share her enjoyment in the pleasures of the ride.

Maria had come to my training course because she felt there

was something wrong in the way she was handling her horse. He seemed so utterly depressed and uninterested in his surroundings, particularly when he was going out for a ride. As soon as I saw her horse however, the problem became clear. She was blaming herself and her training when the difficulties were caused by a mismatch of personalities.

Maria's horse, a dark bay gelding, had been imported from Poland and prior to her ownership had been a school horse. His personality was a lusterless one, partially because of his previous dreary environment, but also because of an innate introversion and dullness.

I noted that his nostrils were very narrow and showed minimal movement. His ears, too, showed little movement, and his eyes, narrowly spaced, deeply set and rather small, had an inward expression — he did not look around or evince any interest in his surroundings. He had a small jowl, a rather longish, narrow head and a short mouth with thick lips. Given all these indications, I thought his intelligence was clearly below average.

"This horse is simply not suited to you," I said. I suggested she sell him and buy a horse whose history wasn't one of complete domination, but who had been encouraged to have a joyful personality, possibly an Arab or Arabian-type horse who would enjoy trail riding as much as she did. Maria was truly relieved to hear that she could stop struggling to "make it right," and could give herself permission to buy a new horse without feeling guilty.

In selling her horse, I suggested to Maria that she look for a buyer who would be quite happy with him, a type of rider who would be happy with a horse who was obedient and not curious about his surroundings.

If this was not possible, I suggested that she retire the horse to pasture, something I've recommended over the years to other people in similar situations.

In a similar case, I received photos for evaluation of a dressage horse who was so unresponsive and resistant that his handler, a professional rider and trainer, was losing confidence in her abilities.

Well, no wonder you're feeling frustrated, I wrote her. This horse has a slight Roman nose, three swirls, short ears set very close together, very narrow nostrils, small eyes and a very short mouthline. In short, the horse is dull, resistant and inflexible. Find someone who just wants to go down the road, or simply wants to ride for exercise and not for companionship or top performance.

The woman was as relieved as Maria to find that there was a perfectly good reason for her to sell the horse, and that the choice to do so did not reflect on her skill as a trainer. I've noticed that many people go through great difficulties making the decision to part with a horse, feeling guilty or at fault, and I find that the ability to evaluate personality is very helpful in such cases.

While Maria herself clearly needed a horse with a lively temperament more closely akin to her own, picking a horse who has similar personality traits to yours may not always be the best choice. I've noticed that people who are high strung, nervous and sensitive are often drawn to horses with the same attributes. In this scenario of like-attracts-like, the mutual nervousness of horse and rider heightens tension, particularly if the rider is not experienced. For such a person, the best match would probably be a horse who is steady and kind.

Getting the right combination of horse and owner is like a game of mix and match, and often what is one person's frustration can be another person's challenge. Let's take, for an example, a horse that has a bump between the eyes like a headlight (unpredictability), an extreme dish face (over-sensitivity), and a pronounced moose nose (boldness). Needless to say, this unusual and contradictory combination of characteristics adds up to a very complex and difficult personality. It is, in fact, the very brew that confronted me a few years ago as I gazed at a photo that I received in the mail for analysis.

The letter enclosed with the photo was from Doris Churchill, a woman who had attended a nine-month course at my residential school for riding instructors in the 1960's. Now Carrie, her 15-year-old daughter, was in her last year of junior showing, without experiencing much success. She was an ambitious young rider, very keen to win.

The only trouble was that Carrie felt herself to be in a double bind. While she loved her horse, he was a complex creature who shied inexplicably and whose unpredictable behavior was often frustrating for the young girl. She never knew how he would be from one show to the next. The question Doris posed to me: Should the horse be sold so that Carrie could find success with a more reasonable horse, or was it worth persevering and working with this particular gelding?

The photo told me everything I needed to know to answer her question. A horse with such an array of difficult characteristics was not a good bet for Carrie. This complicated type needed someone who was not interested in winning, but who was also complex and would enjoy devoting plenty of time to figuring out and working with this horse's particular intricacies of personality. I suggested Doris go out and find a better match for Carrie.

Carrie's horse would have been perfect for someone like Elizabeth Blake. Liz, a very individualistic and fascinating, redheaded Scotswoman living in Arizona, was the owner of a mare, Diva. At one time president of her own marketing company, Liz was successful enough to retire at a relatively young age, so she had plenty of time for Diva, and her grand passion.

Diva is a horse you could describe as Mary, Mary Quite Contrary, but for Liz, who is a born problem solver, she was perfect. The more difficulties the horse presented, the more fascinated

Liz became. The mare was so exceptional, so smart, fiery, proud and moody that I would never recommend her for anyone but a very unusual person, someone who would be both an experienced rider and complex enough to understand and enjoy her subtleties and her need to be treated with utmost respect.

In the hands of the average person, Diva would be a very frustrating handful — disagreeable, resistant, stubborn and full of fight. Liz, however, both knows and intuits exactly how to bring out the best in her, handling the horse with just the right sensitive balance of calm firmness and open-minded respect, a combination which acknowledges the mare's extraordinary and highly individual mind.

To watch Diva and Liz, to see the subtle layers of sympathy at work between them, is to witness the proverbial "match made in heaven."

Of course Liz is a confident and expert rider. What if you're nature is timid, or perhaps you possess confidence but your experience is limited? I remember a case in which a single horse became a challenge for a family where all these factors were present.

Lothar Karla is a friend of mine who owns an international bus company. He's clever, athletic, keenly competitive and kind. To my mind, Lothar has an ideal private stabling facility — a row of large, airy stalls where the horses can hang their heads out for a view of their big sand paddock. They can also be turned out all day, joining a flock of sheep in a large, sun-filled meadow. The humans looking out of the windows in Lothar's house are lucky, too: They get to gaze at this peaceful, pastoral scene and listen to the call of the cuckoos sounding from the nearby forest.

Until the events in the following story, Lothar's main interest in matters equine was to provide horses for the pleasure of his wife, Amanda, and their daughter, Eva.

One day, however, Lothar saw an advertisement in his local paper: "Free horse to good home, come and get it." He had been looking for a horse for his family, so the three of them went to investigate. They found Merik, a big, chestnut warmblood with a bright, broad blaze face and hind stockings, and brought him home.

The trouble was that Merik intimidated Amanda, who was not very confident, and Eva, who was more assured but had little experience with such a large horse. Every time they attempted to enter his stall to feed him, he would pin back his ears and run them right back out.

After three days of this routine, Lothar stepped in. "This is ridiculous," he said. "I'm not going to feed such a horse." He entered the stall himself — armed with a large stick he had plucked from a tree branch — and when the horse tried his usual tactic, Lothar gave him a solid whack on the top of the croup, and then stood his ground and calmly waited for Merik's next move.

Merik jumped away, turned around and faced Lothar with an expression that said, "Wow. Here, finally, is an interesting person." He pricked up his ears and came over to investigate. And that was that for both horse and man; Merik had become Lothar's horse. Lothar, who had originally had no intention of involving himself with Merik, was now the only one to ride him. They had become a dynamic duo.

Merik's head showed a character as strong, self-aware and bright as any I have ever seen. He was extremely broad and flat between the eyes and had a very large jowl and a large, unusually intelligent eye. He had enormous nostrils, a moose nose and a very sloping muzzle.

Here was a horse I felt confident could think faster than a lot of people, a personality who was full of ideas. Lothar once caught him carrying a sheep around with his teeth just to amuse himself. He entertained the whole family, but he always remained Lothar's horse.

Six months later I was invited to meet Merik and to bring Amanda a more suitable horse I had especially chosen for her — a wonderful, very cooperative, baby-sitter-type Quarter Horse from California who was exactly right for her somewhat hesitant nature and who wound up making her very happy. Lothar also bought a horse for Eva, a young, intelligent, confident Arabian, just the thing to match the exuberant energy of this bright young girl herself.

Horses As Teachers

When you really love a horse who also happens to have an extremely difficult personality, it creates a situation that can be, to say the least, most discouraging. I've repeatedly seen people in such a predicament continue to struggle on and on, even though no real progress is being made. The sensible thing to do would be to "just let go."

For most people, I tend to recommend a "guilt-free" parting as the best solution. There are times, however, when persistence is not only in order, it can also become the road to a truly rewarding journey of discovery.

I remember just such an instance. The horse in question was a four-year-old Paso Fino gelding named Hero. When his owner, Marcia Ukura sent me his photos for personality analysis, I thought, "This has got to be one of the most difficult and complex heads I've ever seen."

The first thing that struck me was his sloped-off muzzle, indicating a horse who tests his rider constantly. Added to this was a large nostril (a horse who thinks a lot), a long mouth and a long, flat chin (again a horse who is mentally more active than usual, who can be overly sensitive and easily misunderstood), a quirk bump (unpredictable, quirky behavior), and ears that were fluted and rotated slightly sideways like antennae, as though the horse didn't quite trust his environment (photo 1).

In the letter Marcia sent with the photos, she described her level of experience as well as her problems with Hero: "I have been riding for three years, taking lessons the whole time; a year of western, a year of hunt seat and a year taking lessons on Hero with an instructor for Saddlebred horses.

"Hero's training started when he was 34 months old and lasted three months, after which he was shown successfully in both Fino and Performance classes. When I first began riding him I warmed him up in an arena and then took him out on the trail. After two months he became very unruly, refused to walk, wanted to go as fast as he could at all times, and would start rearing and spinning when I wouldn't let him go at his own pace.

"I resumed his training and had lessons on him once a week. After several months he was almost perfect, performing all three gaits correctly (even four-beat gait), and responsive to the bit, but touchy at the sides, so my leg cues had to be almost nothing.

"Six weeks later, I rode on the trail again. He was once more completely crazy, rearing, spinning when restrained and changing gaits so fast it made my head spin trying to figure out what he was doing.

"I put him back in training with a third trainer, someone quite experienced with Paso Finos, and she told me that he liked to get himself worked up and that it was difficult for him to relax.

"He is my first horse and I love him dearly. I don't want another horse. Can a middle-aged, arthritic woman learn to get along with this horse?"

I called up Marcia and said, "Look, if you want to learn more than you've ever learned in your life, keep this horse. He'll be a tremendous challenge and you may come out fine in the end. On the other hand, if you don't want a whole lot of trouble, pass him along to someone who does and get yourself a horse who takes care of you. That's the choice you have to make."

Marcia attended one of my clinics and was utterly amazed at the changes in behavior that our TTEAM techniques brought about in several of the horses. She went home and with the help of a sympathetic and competent instructor, she began all over again with Hero, this time using our TTEAM training methods.

Two months later we had a glowing letter from Marcia: "I work with him four times a week. He always gets a TTouch body treatment and some part of the ground exercises. The difference in his behavior is amazing — not always as amazing as I'd like it to be, but amazing nevertheless.

"We board in an equestrian center and there is no quiet place to do TTEAM work so Hero had to learn self-control. When we first started, he would stand in cross ties stomping his feet and swinging from side to side. Now, he stands quietly in the aisle for his treatment, nude, without cross ties or halter, while horses, people and dogs mill all around us.

"Prior to starting the TTEAM work, cutting a bridle path was a two person, halter and chain job that was a real struggle. Now I just touch his poll and he lowers his head while I trim.

"Hero and I are learning to work together with voice commands. He requires very loud, commanding voice cues. Whenever I try to soften my voice he soon begins to take advantage of me and do what he wants instead of what I want. I think I'm getting the upper hand because I can lead him all over the barn, in and out of the wash stall, into small areas, backward and forward, without any tack, just my hands on his bare head.

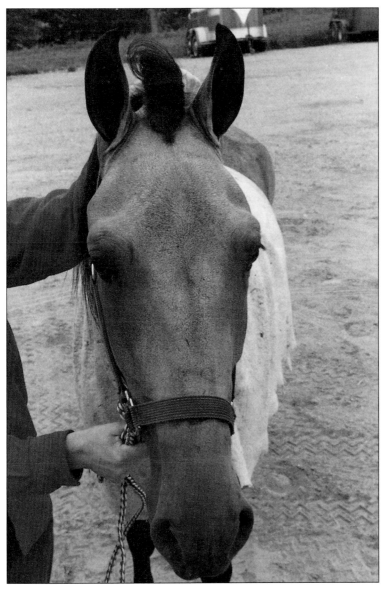

1. Hero. Observe the extreme narrowness between the ears, the very unusual angle from the eye up to the ear, and the narrowness of the face in the section from below the eyes to the flare of the nostrils.

"I can do everything with him except the TTEAM hind leg exercises (see page 168). The minute I try to move the hind legs around he turns me off. It's as if he doesn't know where they are and is afraid to find out. I keep doing the exercise but it's difficult when the horse can't relax with this and doesn't cooperate. His tail is much looser though. Is there something I can do?"

I advised her to do small, connected Clouded Leopard (see page 153) circles going over the croup, the hock and all the way down the hind legs to get him used to getting his hind legs handled. Also I suggested she let him stand with one toe resting on the ground while she did the circles.

Hero was just about as difficult a horse as you can get for a beginner, but such horses can be wonderful teachers — sometimes you can learn more about horses working on a difficult horse than you can from a horse who is perfectly cooperative and has no problems.

Because Hero was such a strong character, he forced Marcia to "take the reins" and become more assured herself. To cope with him intelligently, she had to develop new levels of personal self-confidence, stretching her own abilities and reinforcing positive qualities within her own personality. For Marcia, "lessons with Hero" wound up affecting and enriching all aspects of her own life — a delightful end for a story that began with frustration and feelings of helplessness and ended with patience and love.

A challenging horse like Hero can teach a rider that an understanding approach can be much more powerful than force or punishment. Such an approach brings with it an exhilarating sense of accomplishment and the very real joy that comes with cooperation between human and horse.

Matchmaking

Socks, a 19-year-old Quarter Horse gelding, carries his 75-year-old physician owner out on the trail with extraordinary awareness and care. You can see what a good match he is for an old gentleman (photos 2 & 3).

2. Socks. A "caretaker" gelding, has a very straight profile (uncomplicated) and squarish muzzle (dependability).

3. Front view: Note that Socks has very broad ears, medium length and rather undefined, which mark him as totally reliable, and his exceptionally mobile "prehensile" lip, which makes him look as though he can get a good grasp on any situation.

4. The most striking characteristics about Duchess are her small eye and absent expression, her Roman head and the rather strange tightness around her lips, as though she is sucking her tongue. This shot was taken when she was in a very unhappy situation, pushed beyond her capacity.

5. Three months later: Duchess and her new owner, Minty Flood, demonstrate the power of love — the mare's eye is soft, her chin more relaxed.

Two photographs of Duchess, a nine-year-old warmblood mare, were taken three months apart (photos 4 & 5).

At the time the first photo was taken, the mare's previous owner was longeing Duchess hard and fast for 45 minutes each day prior to jumping her over large fences. Under this kind of pressure the horse was not able to give what was asked and became so nervous under saddle that the trainer recommended selling her.

She was sold to Minty Flood, whose approach to horses is open hearted and caring. With Minty, Duchess was able to develop trust in her rider, and she now has the self-confidence to jump fences that would have been a major problem for her in her earlier situation.

The first step in successful "equine matchmaking" is analysis of what you, the prospective owner, need from a horse. Once you are clear on what you want a horse *for*, and what would be an appropriate character match for your own temperament, you've got your parameters set.

Knowing whether you want a horse for a particular discipline or just for pleasure will influence the way you look at prospective horses. For instance, if you want a tough polo pony, or a horse for any discipline that demands focus, confidence and stability, then you know that a horse with a dish face is almost certainly inappropriate. If, on the other hand, you want a horse who will be your companion on the trail for pleasure, then you have a great deal more leeway when faced with the choice of a wide variety of equine characteristics.

However, even with the purchase of a horse just for pleasure and not for show, you should be clear in your mind about the sort of horse you want. Let's say you're a social rider and you just want to have a good time with a few friends. What you may be looking for are characteristics that point to a steady and reliable steed. But if you enjoy a horse that is curious and eager to see what's over the next hill, you should be on the lookout for different traits.

Should you desire a horse for a particular discipline, you'll have to pay special attention not only to mental and emotional tendencies, but also to the structure of the body, making sure the horse is physically capable of giving you what you want. Just as humans do, horses differ in their capacities to perform certain sports; their conformation may help or hinder them. Certainly, you wouldn't ask a sumo wrestler to run a marathon, nor would you ask a short-muscled horse to win a 100-mile endurance ride.

The question of weight should also be considered. Most people don't think of how important it can be in determining the suitability of horse to rider. I first became aware of this question of weight at Canadian horse shows in the 1950s where the hunter classes had divisions based on the horse's weight carrying abilities. Hunters were termed lightweight, middleweight and heavyweight, as determined by the circumference of the cannon bone directly below the knee, and the circumference of the girth.

The consideration of weight when matching horse and rider makes sense, not only for hunters but for all breeds, as I've often seen cases where owner and horse are mismatched in weight, causing many behavioral and physical problems.

An example: An Arabian gelding was brought to one of my clinics because of his resistant behavior. He was absolutely miserable, pinned his ears when anyone approached him and was generally depressed, dull and unwilling. Now this horse, about 14.3 hands, was definitely in the lightweight class; he was small and very light boned, yet he was being ridden by a woman who weighed in at over 220 pounds. We put a much lighter rider on him and the result was predictable. The gelding went forward willingly and lost his depressed demeanor. His rider had not realized that her weight was causing the problem. Now she had a difficult decision to make — whether to sell the gelding and find a more suitable horse for her weight, or to keep her horse and drive him instead.

To be fair, it is useful to assess whether you and a horse are the right "weight match." Make sure you are not too heavy, but also understand that you may be too light. I have seen cases in which short and light riders choose 1,300-pound, 17-hand warmblood types they are then unable to control, because horse and rider are not suited in weight and height.

When evaluating a horse for a match, I recommend that you write down your impressions of him in an orderly way. Begin by jotting down your step by step analysis of the horse's head and body. Then itemize those characteristics that appeal to you and those that do not. Consider carefully whether the horse is cooperative, likes to learn, and is physically, mentally and emotionally capable of doing the required job.

You may already own the horse, but that should not stop you from periodically questioning your match and observing him as closely as you would a prospective purchase. Ask yourself: Am I enjoying my association with this horse? Do I really take pleasure in his training and the time I spend with him?

Maybe you are having difficulties. In that case, question yourself to see if you are asking too much too fast from your horse. Re-examine your training methods. Stop and take time to evaluate your horse to see whether he is really suitable for the level of performance you are seeking. Consider your horse's physical, mental and emotional capacities — the limitations of his personality as well as his strengths.

As you're working with your horse you might sometimes get discouraged, thinking, "Oh, she'll never change," or, "This doesn't really seem to be making any difference." I know everyone feels like that sometimes — certainly I have. One way, however, to improve your training technique, is to replace your negative outlook with positive mental imaging.

There is ample evidence that mental imaging does affect physical outcomes. In every sport, the practice of positive visualization has become an accepted tool for success. As verified cases accumulate, the medical profession, too, has acknowledged the transformative power of visualization and its beneficial and sometimes miraculous effect on disease.

Our expectations can have a strong influence on the outcome of our efforts. I've seen this demonstrated repeatedly in working with horses, who can respond positively or negatively depending on how we perceive them.

As you work with your horse, you can improve his performance by imagining him as you'd like him to be. You may find yourself delightfully surprised to see the extraordinary difference your expectation makes in speeding up and effecting a shift in personality.

In the end, there are many conclusions you can draw. You might discover that understanding your horse from a new point of view gives you the ability to work out any problems you have been encountering. Instead of blaming yourself for training failures, you may realize that it's your horse who has a specific difficulty or limitation, one that you can help him overcome with easy methods of retraining.

Over and over again, I see cases in which a person is drawn to a horse that really is unsuitable, but because it was love at first sight, he or she is not going to give up easily. Sometimes, when a person sticks with a difficult horse, the horse will, in the end, lead the rider to a completely new way of thinking. As you work together to overcome the difficulties, these very difficulties can become doors that open to new horizons. It is, after all, not the destination, but the journey itself that matters.

I hope that this book will hone your powers of observation, adding a whole new dimension to the way you view horses and the art of horsemanship.

CHAPTER NINE

TTEAM: Some Tools for Change

During the 1970's, when I taught classes on equine personality, I never thought about influencing or changing equine character. I remember reading an article about nervous horses and how they could not be changed, and I recall a well known Olympic rider saying to his students, "Once a biter, always a biter." However, as we began to develop the system of equine training we now call TTEAM, it became clear to me that particular techniques and exercises actually did work to change or modify innate characteristics. To my surprise, I found that working on a horse's body in specific ways — releasing fear, discomfort or pain in the body, and improving a horse's ability to learn through carefully orchestrated ground exercises — could, and indeed did, influence personality.

TEAM is an acronym for the Tellington-Jones Equine Awareness Method, the special system of training for horses and riders that has been developing for two decades. Inspired by my years of study and work with the techniques of Dr. Moshe Feldenkrais, I first developed the TEAM ground exercises. Later, drawing on my interest in cellular intelligence and my previous experience with equine massage and physical therapy, I added the Tellington TTouch. The double T in TTEAM represents the blend of TEAM and TTouch that we now use as a method of training and healing horses for optimal performance and health.

TTEAM ground exercises influence behavioral and physical problems by dramatically expanding and improving a horse's capacity for learning and cooperation, and by improving balance and coordination.

The Tellington TTouch is a series of circular touches of the hands and fingers intended to activate cellular function and to further deeper communication and understanding between horse and trainer. For each TTouch, hands and fingers are held in different positions and applied with varied pressure, depending on the effect desired.

The TTouch is used to encourage and increase relaxation, improve athletic ability, introduce a new sense of awareness, enhance healing and reduce stress in performance horses.

In the following pages you'll find a selection of TTouches, body exercises to get started with TTEAM and TTEAM ground exercises that we hope will assist you in bringing out the best in your horse.

Using the Tellington TTouch

The Circles

The instructions for the basic TTouch are fairly simple. The foundation for the TTouch is a circular movement called the Clouded Leopard. It is the first TTouch we teach because the techniques and principles used are basic to all the circular TTouches.

Begin by orienting yourself: Imagine the face of a quarter-sized clock anywhere on your horse's body. With your left hand placed lightly on your horse, take your right hand and place the fingers at six o'clock on the bottom of the circle of your imaginary dial. With your fingers held in a lightly curved position like a paw, push the skin around the face of your imaginary clock in a circle and a quarter and release. Maintain an even, constant pressure from six o'clock all the way around the clock face past six, until you reach eight o'clock. At eight pause for a second, and if the animal seems to be relaxed with the contact, bring your fingers away softly and begin again at another spot chosen at random. The hand and arm should be relaxed and flexible. When concentrating it is natural to hold your breath and thereby stiffen the fingers causing the horse to tense rather than relax, so remember to keep breathing rhythmically.

Generally we use a clockwise circle, which tends to integrate and strengthen the horse. However, if we are dealing with a horse who is resistant or who is very tense, we sometimes begin with counter clockwise circles (which release tension) and then switch to clockwise after the horse calms.

In the basic TTouch, we place the circles at random as a way of keeping the horse focused. He remains in a state of attention because he is wondering where the next move will come from. Because each circle is a complete movement within itself, you can work the body in any order you wish without losing effectiveness.

Once your horse begins to accept the TTouch, follow a line running parallel to your horse's top line and connect each circle with a light slide about two inches between circles.

It's important to make only *one circle and a quarter at a time* on any one spot. Practically anyone learning the TTouch has a natural tendency at first to keep circling over the same place. Oddly, most people seem instinctively to make three consecutive circles. The usual effect this has, however, is to irritate the horse.

When you make the circle, use your thumb as a steadying base and move your middle three fingers softly as one. Allow the little finger to follow softly. Keep the joints in your fingers rounded rather than straight, allowing them to relax and move with the rotation. To see the difference in effect, make a circle on yourself holding the fingers stiffly and then make the same circle with the joints of your fingers, particularly the first joints, softened. It's much easier with the joints mobile, isn't it?

In working the TTouch it's important to make sure that your circles are really round and that they are made in one smooth flowing movement.

If, when you make your initial circles, your horse moves around, make the circles fairly fast, taking about one second to make each circular motion. As your horse begins to trust and enjoy what's happening, as you feel him begin to enter a state of bodily "listening," slow each circle down to approximately three seconds. To complete this slower circle, instead of simply lifting off when you reach eight o'clock, pause, and allow your fingers to come up in a gradual release, as though a sponge were slowly pushing them up and away from the body. Then slide to the next circle.

The first, more speedy circle awakens the body. The second, slower approach releases muscular tension, enhances breathing, and gives you a key to deeper communication.

Pressure

One of the most common questions I hear about the TTouch is, "Don't you get tired doing this work?"

No, I say, if your hand gets tired or your horse remains nervous, your technique needs improvement. Effective pressure is related not to muscle power but to how you hold your hands and to consciously remembering to breathe softly and easily.

Most of the time our intent with the TTouch is to awaken the cells, and you don't have to be a body builder to exert the right pressure. There are times, however, when you'll want to go deeper into the body with your TTouches, for example with a horse who has a laid-back personality.

The TTouch employs a pressure scale from one to 10. To learn the measure of each number, begin with number one as your guideline. To practice and learn the difference between pressures, bring your right hand up to your face, steadying the bent right elbow against your body with your other hand. (Do the reverse, of course, if you're left handed.)

Then, placing your thumb against your cheek in order to give your hand support, with the tip of your middle finger push the skin on your eyelid around in a circle with the lightest possible contact. (If you are wearing contact lenses, use caution.) Take your finger away and repeat to get a sense of just how very light that lightest TTouch feels.

Next, on the fleshy part of your left forearm, make a circle using the same pressure you used on your eyelid, and observe how little indentation you make in the skin. That lightest circular pressure is number one.

To find pressure number three, repeat the process, only this time push the skin on your eyelid around in a circle as firmly as is comfortably possible. (I always emphasize the word "comfortably" and tell my students, "The idea isn't to pop out your eyeball.") Then, retaining the sense memory of that pressure, go once again to your forearm to see how the TTouch feels there and to confirm the pressure by observing the depth of indentation in the muscle. Staying with your forearm now, go back to the one pressure and compare it with the three. Note the difference in feel and depth of indentation.

A pressure two times deeper is a six and three times deeper into the muscle is a number nine or 10. When pressures above seven are done with the pads of the fingers they can cause tension and discomfort to both doer and receiver, whereas if you tip your fingers upright so the first digit is standing at 90 degrees to the horse's body, you can lead with your nails and penetrate deeply into the muscle with no discomfort (see Bear TTouch page 156).

You'll find yourself experimenting with pressure until you click into the one that is right for the horse you're working with. Horses that are more heavily muscled may be more responsive to the deeper pressures. If they have any sort of pain or inflammation you may have to work with a two to four pressure.

While the basics I've outlined here may seem complicated on paper, they are actually surprisingly easy to learn. After a little bit of practice, you'll find yourself using the TTouch naturally, intuitively, and, let's not forget, pleasurably.

The Clouded Leopard

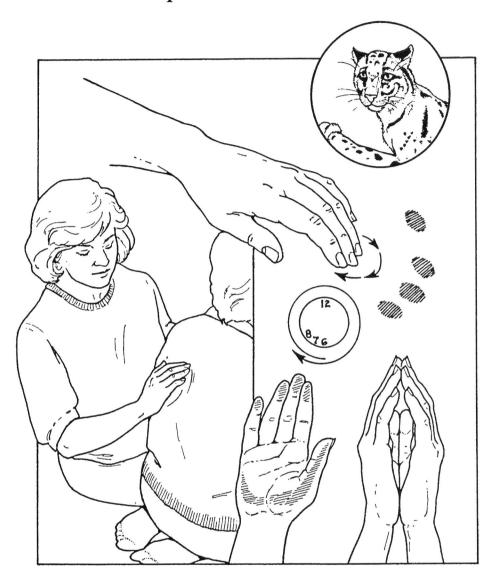

When:

The basic TTouch is the Clouded Leopard. The "cloud" part of the name describes the lightness with which the whole hand contacts the body (lightly as a cloud), and the "leopard" stands for the range of pressure of the fingers. A leopard can be very light on his feet as in the light TTouch of a one, two or three, or very strong, as in the six to nine pressure scale. The stronger Leopard TTouch is appropriate for the more heavily muscled or blocked horse.

How:

Hold the hand gently curved and using the pads of the fingers, do the circles as described on page 150.

The Lying Leopard

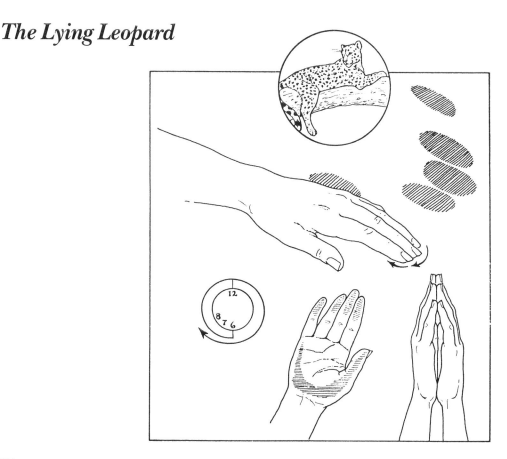

When:

This TTouch is good for a particularly sensitive horse when the Clouded Leopard is considered too invasive or threatening. It's good, too, to reduce the pain and possible swelling of injuries.

How:

For this TTouch, the Leopard lies down, i.e., the curve of the hand flattens somewhat, allowing a larger portion of warm contact. Remember to keep the joints of your fingers slightly rounded. Doing so will maintain a softness in your hand, arm and shoulder that will help you to keep your breathing quiet and rhythmic.

If the horse is nervous or doesn't want to be touched, make the circles faster, and slow down as he relaxes. As you slow down become aware of making the circle round and really feel the skin under your fingers.

Compare the feeling of the Lying Leopard and the Clouded Leopard on your own arm to help you see and feel the difference and to know when to use each one.

The Lying Leopard TTouch is one that I often use for fresh injuries to reduce the pain and the possibility of swelling. When an area is really painful or injured, very lightly cup your hand over the wounded area and move the skin in a circle with a two pressure, keeping the raised, cupped portion of your hand directly over the injury.

Do this to yourself and note the sensation: It should impart a protective feeling. If the area is too painful to approach immediately, make gentle slow, tiny circles all around the injury first, before cupping your hand over it. Sometimes it is necessary to TTouch the corresponding area on the other side of the body to gain trust. If the wound is open and you have first aid equipment available, place a sterile covering over the wound before approaching it.

The Raccoon

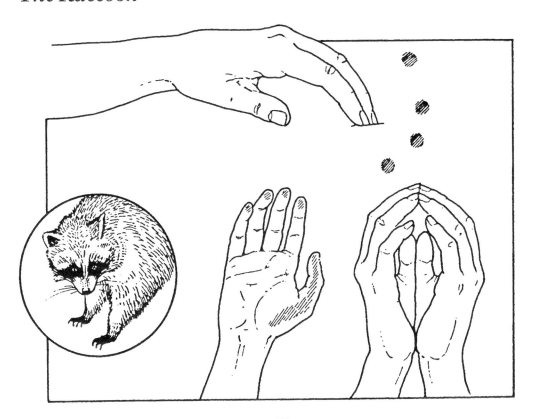

When:

The Raccoon TTouch is named after the tiny, delicate movements of a raccoon washing its food. Its special uses are for delicate work, for working around small areas, to speed up the healing of wounds and reduce swelling without causing pain, and to increase circulation and activate neural impulses in the lower legs.

How:

Contact using the lightest possible pressure, using the tips of the fingers just behind the nails.

The Bear

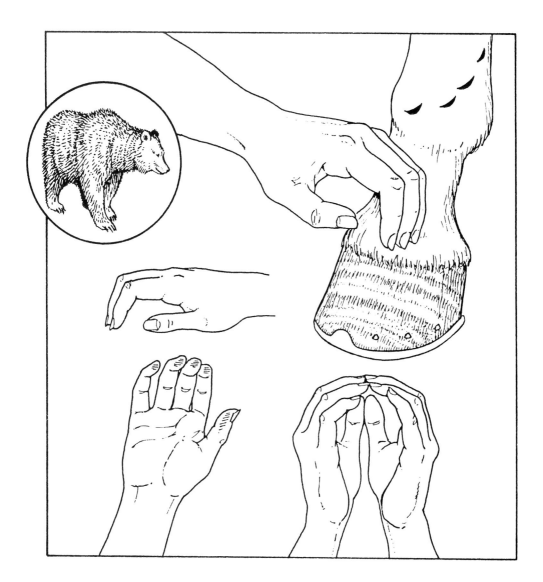

When:

The Bear TTouch allows the fingers to move deeply into areas of heavy muscling without discomfort to the recipient or the practitioner.

How:

Your fingernails should be of medium length, about one-eighth of an inch long, so that when you direct your fingertips straight down the recipient can feel the nails rather than the pads. Make your complete circle with your fingertips in this "straight down" position. In the muscled areas, the TTouch should feel as though you are parting the layers, not "digging" into the muscle itself.

The Flick of the Bear's Paw

When:

This is a useful TTouch for approaching a horse who is fearful of contact. We also use it for performance horses who have been worked with the TTouch just before entering the arena. After the calming effect of a TTouch session, the Flick of the Bear's Paw wakes up the body and alerts the horse without creating nervousness. If you don't complete the session this way, your horse can be too relaxed to perform well.

How:

This TTouch is a brushing stroke that is used in long lines starting at the top of the neck and continuing on down the neck, over the shoulders, back and hindquarters. The motion reminds me of a bear fishing for salmon or a person brushing lint off clothing. The amount of pressure used in this TTouch will vary from horse to horse. Some like vigorous movement and contact while others prefer a very light, almost grazing TTouch, as though you were brushing them with a feather. Use your wrists flexibly as you skip from place to place on the body. The horse may move around a bit at first but generally will soon become quiet.

Noah's March

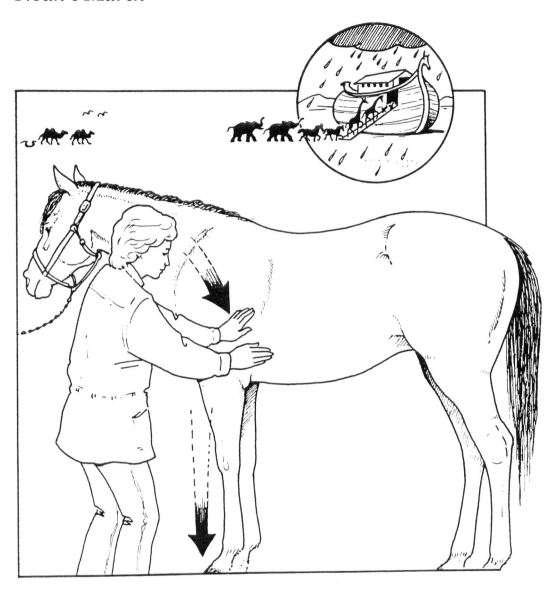

When:

This long, firm stroke of the hand over all of the body is used to complete a TTouch session. After the experience of revivification that the TTouch has brought to individual parts of the body, Noah's March brings back a sense of wholeness and re-integration.

How:

Begin at the head and make firm, long strokes. Cover every inch of the body as though you were cutting hay.

Back Lifts

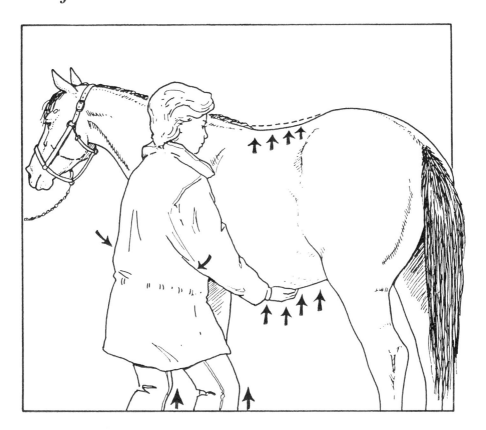

The back lift changes the relationship of the vertebrae and allows the horse to lower and lengthen the neck.

When:

Back Lifts are useful in the following cases:

- to lower the head;
- to give the horse a way of activating the belly muscles and experiencing a new feeling in the back;
- for sway backs;
- for ewe necks;
- to fill out the hollow places in the back and withers whenever a horse drops his back, as after saddling and mounting;
- for a horse who is sensitive to grooming;
- for a mare heavy with foal;
- for an older horse whose back has dropped.

How:

The illustration shows the fingertips with nails being used in a quick press-and-release motion near the midline of the belly starting behind the front legs. Be sure to start gently at first to avoid being kicked. Once your horse learns to raise the back to fingernail pressure, you'll find that simply stroking upward from the belly line with your fingertips spread apart will get the same results.

If the horse is sensitive, start with the Clouded Leopard TTouch along the midline.

Exploring Your Horse's Body for Pain and Stress

The TTouch for Exploration

The TTEAM TTouch and Pressure Exploration is used to check the tension of a horse and to discover, through eliciting physical symptoms, the stress or pain that might be affecting personality.

The best way to start out a TTEAM exploration is with a Bear TTouch. In using the Bear TTouch for exploration, the fingertips and nails, held slightly bent like a fish hook, press in quickly and release. Begin with a number five pressure, then you can move in either direction in the pressure scale to discover the range that is most suitable. If you are using as mild a pressure as a number three pressure yet your horse still attempts to kick, bite or move away, it could be an indication of an over-reactive horse due to hormone imbalance, a horse who has been unfairly punished and is fearful, a nervous and flighty horse, or a horse who is actually sore and in pain.

In such a case, switch to the Lying Leopard TTouch with a two or three pressure to give a warm, reassuring feeling. The fear and discomfort will usually disappear. With a number five pressure for exploration, a healthy horse will show a slight response but no fear or spasm.

Taking a case at the opposite end of the scale — let's say you increase the pressure to a nine or even a 10 and yet the horse's response remains sluggish and minimal. The appropriate step to take in this case would be to penetrate more deeply into the areas of the body that are insensitive. With this penetrating pressure, you are actually giving the cells an opportunity to feel and the nervous system a chance to respond, thereby increasing the horse's sensitivity. Often, it can take as little as 10 minutes of deep TTouch to make your horse very sensitive in the next session, so don't overdo deep TTouches.

Procedure for Exploration

To explore your horse's body and find the greatest areas of sensitivity or soreness, start the exploration at the neck in the middle of the large muscles just behind the ears. Stand in front of your horse's head and stroke him with the flat of your hand first, so you don't surprise him, and then go in with your Bear TTouch, using both hands, one on either side of the neck. You may get a very strong response at first, because the horse is not expecting the sensation, so you may want to stroke once more before you try again.

The TTouch for Exploration: Various parts of the body are outlined on Elena Petreshkova's Russian stallion, winner of an Olympic Gold Medal. These outlines can be used to help you locate the areas to be explored with the TTouch.

Move down the neck, and to the shoulders, still pressing from both sides. After you have explored the shoulders, move to the side, and though you cannot explore both sides at once, be sure to "support" with one hand while using the exploratory TTouch with the other. Your "supporting" hand is placed on the "off" side of the horse, just on the other side of the spine.

Be careful to watch for your horse's response, which, if your horse is very sensitive or sore, could be a strong threat, a kick or a bite. Remember, that's his way of "talking" to you, so listen and always be alert. Finish your exploration with a firm stroke to integrate the body between TTouches.

Getting Started with TTEAM

This step-by-step, beginner's guide was the "brain-child" of my sister, Robyn Hood. Robyn is as inseparable from the development of TTEAM as bark from a growing tree. She is a brilliantly innovative and perceptive teacher of TTEAM, who amidst the press of her own life raising children and breeding and selling Icelandic horses, also manages to produce our TTEAM Newsletter. Robyn's creative input and discernment is a vital element in the refinement of TTEAM methods, as with time and experience, we continue to evolve new and improved techniques.

The trainer in the following series of photographs is Robyn, photographed working her horse, Buddha, by her husband, Phil Pretty.

One of the most effective ways to use TTEAM is to integrate the "tools" into your everyday way of working with a horse. Even if you do not use the specific methods, your attitude and way of perceiving your horse will help you relate in a different way.

The easiest place to start is when you are grooming. If you groom your horse on cross-ties, check to see at what height they are set. If the cross-ties are set so that the horse's head is held up and cannot be lowered allowing the neck to be level, he will not benefit as much from the grooming. When the head is held high, the back will have a tendency to drop down when brushed. We recommend teaching your horse to stand still for grooming without being tied.

Allowing the horse to maintain an effective head position is important to physical, emotional and mental balance. In addition, the TTEAM process of teaching the horse to lower his head on cue:

- overrides the flight, fight or freeze reflex;
- relieves muscle tension in the neck and the back;
- encourages rhythmical breathing;
- establishes the handler at a higher "pecking order" position than the horse without using force.

There are two tools we use with TTEAM, a four-foot-long dressage whip (we call a wand) and a 28-inch chain attached to a six-foot nylon lead. The chain is threaded straight into the ring on the left side of the halter, down and then up once over the noseband. Then the chain and snap thread straight out through the ring on the right side, until finally, the snap is attached to the top ring on the right side.

Because so many people have seen a chain used abusively, controversy sometimes arises about our use of it. The way the chain is attached gives the horse a much clearer signal than does a rope attached to the ring under the chin. We do not use the chain to shank the horse; and of course we **never** tie a horse up with the nylon lead if he has the chain on.

The following photographs 1–19 illustrate how to get started with TTEAM bodywork:

1. This is one way to lower a horse's head. First, stroke the horse's neck, chest and legs to accustom him to the wand. Stroking with the wand helps the horse to keep his balance when lowering his head, and aids in relaxing the muscles in his neck. With your fingers held lightly but firmly on the noseband ask your horse to lower his head. Thread a 28-inch chain straight into the ring on the left side of the halter, down and then up once over the noseband and from the inside straight out through the ring on the right side. Attach the snap to the top ring on the right side.

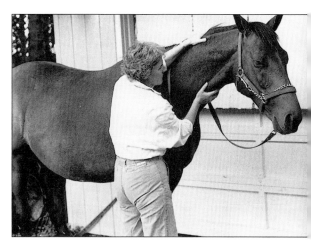

1

2. With your right hand on the crest and your left hand on the nose, ask your horse to lower his head so his poll is level with his withers, or slightly below in the case of a very nervous horse. With the head at this height, I find the horse can relax but still focus and not just "bliss out."

Use your right hand to work with a combination of TTouches. Try the Clouded Leopard by using the pads of your fingers to make single circles at the top of the neck, or lift the crest gently with your fingers and thumb, holding, and slowly releasing.

Using this method to lower the head transfers to when you are riding. If your horse becomes upset and raises his head, reach forward and work his crest in the same way you did from the ground, and he will relax because this has become his habitual response.

By taking a few minutes to lower your horse's head before you groom, you will help him relax and focus more quickly when you get on his back.

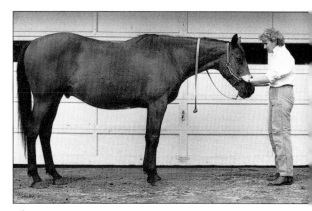

2

3. To help your horse relax between classes at a horse show, try the Neck Rocking. With one hand on the crest and the other on the jugular, gently rock the top and bottom of the neck back and forth. You can see in this photo the horse's eyes are nearly closed.

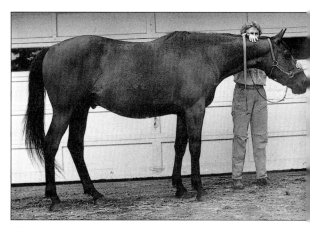

3

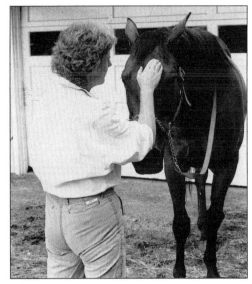

4

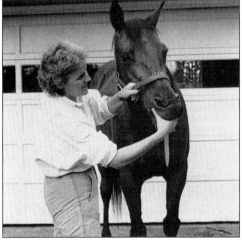

5

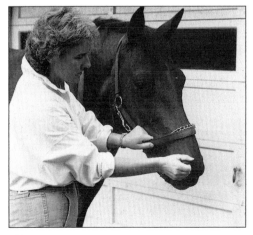

6

4. With your left hand on the noseband of the halter and your right hand on the face, make random, single, clockwise circles on the forehead, around the base of the ears and down the face. Take a couple of minutes to do this and you will help an overly emotional horse stay more focused. Also, it will help you gain a wonderful rapport with your horse. If your horse is head shy, difficult to catch or generally untrusting, this will make a difference in just a few sessions.

5. Working inside the mouth is very helpful for horses who are overly emotional or re-active, who are difficult to bridle, paste worm, twitch or float teeth on, who bite, chew the bit, stick out the tongue, suck the tongue, or grind their teeth. Hold your hand open with your fingers close together. Rub back and forth across the gums where the upper lip meets the gums. If your horse's mouth is dry, wet your hand. Notice the trainer's left hand is holding the halter to stabilize the horse's head. Work the bottom gum as well.

6. Working the nostrils helps a horse to be more tolerant and easier to tube. It encourages relaxation once a horse is used to it. Once again the left hand holds the halter lightly but firmly. Use the heel of your right hand to stroke down in a gentle but firm motion. Too light a pressure will tickle and too firm will irritate.

7. If your horse has trouble lowering his head from the ground or is stiff to the left or right under saddle, try showing him how to bend. Here, the handler's left hand makes small Raccoon TTouch circles on the second cervical vertebra while the right hand guides the horse to turn right. She is asking him, rather than forcing his head.

Many times a horse will swing his hindquarters away rather than bend his neck — not because he is being resistant, but because he is stiff and cannot bend his neck easily and therefore moves his hindquarters instead. If this happens, ask him to give his head less, or perhaps try raising or lowering his head to find a comfortable range to teach the movement. You can also use another method of asking him to bend as described in the next photo.

7

8. As the handler's right hand rests lightly on the horse's right jowl, her left hand guides his head back to the vertical. Starting with the side to which your horse bends more easily, bend him just to the point where he becomes stiff. Then bend the head back to the other side. Repeat this bending several times, each time asking for just a little more bend. Hold a clear picture in your mind of the movement you want and do not force the bend. Be sure to keep the plane of the face perpendicular to the ground. By keeping the plane of the face vertical to the ground the weight is placed more evenly over both front legs which improves both balance and the horse's ability to bend in both directions.

If you spend about five minutes on the head and neck, once or twice a week before riding, you will see improvement under saddle.

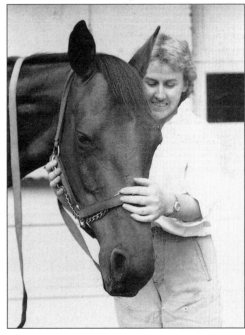

8

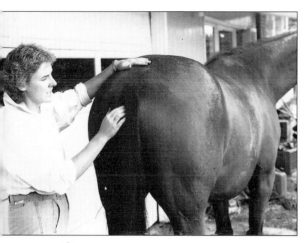

9

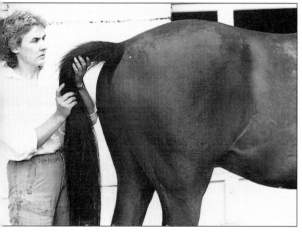

10

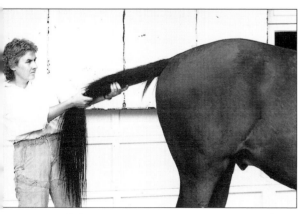

11

The following photos 9–12 illustrate TTEAM tail work which you can incorporate into the grooming routine taking about four minutes. The work with the tail has many benefits. It is a non-habitual movement. Pulling the tail helps horses who are afraid of things behind them and mares before they are bred or before being palpated by the veterinarian. It helps horses engage their hindquarters under saddle by giving them a new sense of awareness of their hindquarters.

9. Use the Raccoon TTouch along the tail-bone, underneath and alongside the point of the buttocks before picking up the tail. If your horse's tail is very clamped, these circles will make the tail work easier.

10. Create an arch by pushing the tailbone with your left hand while pushing the tail toward the horse with your right. Hold the tail in this shape and rotate it in both directions. The upward arch combined with the rotation at the root of the tail is essential to this exercise. It disrupts a habitual pattern of holding in the back and hindquarters of horses who kick or clamp the tail when nervous. It's also one of the few exercises that stops nervous wringing or swishing of the tail. For safety, when first working this movement, do so from the side.

Caution: If your horse has a very loose tail — when you start to pull and there is little resistance, as though the tail is attached with a loose rubber band — pull carefully. In this case, use the position in photo 10 and, besides making circles with the tailbone, gently pull back with the tail curved. Then push the tailbone towards the spine. Also, I would suggest doing more circles at the top of the tailbone of a loose-tailed horse to help him make a better connection to his tail.

11. Slide your hands down the tail and pull, then hold for approximately six seconds and release very slowly. A fast release is counterproductive to this movement. This tail pull seems to open the spine, often causing a horse to take a deep breath.

12. Another way to work the tail is to move each vertebrae up and down like a string of pearls. Here, the handler is pushing in with her thumbs on top of the tailbone as she pulls out with her fingers under the tailbone. Start from the top of the tail downward. You will notice that some vertebrae are more flexible than others.

The following photos 13–19 illustrate TTEAM leg exercises. By doing these exercises, you improve your horse's balance. The improved physical balance then changes your horse's mental and emotional balance.

12

13. When you pick up your horse's feet to clean them, incorporate the TTEAM leg exercises; it doesn't take more than 30 seconds extra per leg. Instead of leaning into your horse's shoulder when picking up his foot, stroke down the leg with your hand and use a squeeze/release motion with your fingernails just above the fetlock joint. This signal teaches the horse to take his weight onto his other legs and to rebalance-balance in order to lift his foot.

14. Here, the handler supports the fetlock joint with her left hand and keeps her left forearm alongside the tendon in order to prevent torquing the knee. (From the right side of the horse, the right hand and forearm would do this.) Her right hand supports the hoof with her thumb on the heel and fingers around the hoof. Her right elbow rests on her right knee, allowing her legs rather than her back to do the work.

Circle the hoof, horizontal to the ground, around the point where that leg would normally be standing. The smooth, round motion of the circle is more important than its size.

In this photo, the leg is coming out to the side and is at a height just below the knee.

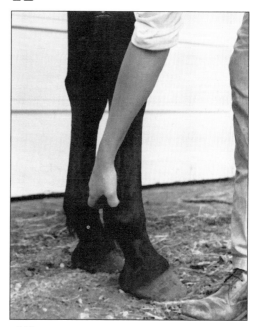

13

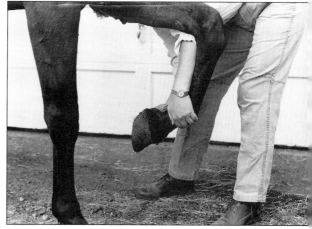

14

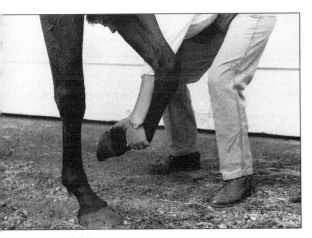

15

16

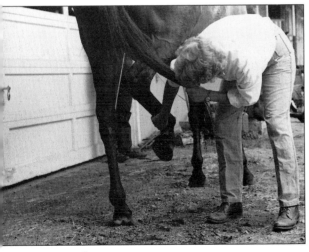

17

15. Here the hoof is coming back behind the other front leg and is about at fetlock height. At each height (knee, mid-cannon, fetlock, pastern) make two circles in one direction and reverse, repeating at the various levels mentioned above.

16. Instead of just putting the hoof down, continue to circle down as close to the ground as you can and tap the toe in a circle on the ground if possible. By resting the toe as shown, the shoulder can release in a non-habitual way. If your horse is very tight in the shoulders or low in the heels, resting the toe may be difficult at first.

With very tense horses you have to build up the ground with a pile of leg quilts or towels for a couple of sessions until they can relax and rest the toe on the ground. Stroking the tendon when the toe is down relaxes the leg and shoulder. Most horses rest the toe only for a moment. This position helps to improve their balance.

17. Stand beside your horse's hind leg rather than with your hip into him. This teaches the horse to keep his balance instead of leaning on his handler. Run your hand down the back of the leg and ask with the same squeeze/release signal for the front leg. If you don't know the horse or if he is difficult, start with one hand holding the tail.

When the horse is tight in the hindquarters or nervous about having the leg held, support the leg in the direction he wants to take it. When you try to take the leg back immediately, the horse only becomes stiffer and more tense.

In this type of situation, try using the TTouch on the hindquarters before picking up the foot. A few minutes of the Raccoon Touch with a four or five pressure on the hindquarters and thigh will help loosen the hindquarters. Also helpful in softening the hindquarters is what we call the Jellyfish Jiggle. Lay your hand flat on the horse's croup and thigh and softly jiggle the muscles.

18. Since most horses expect the handler to hold up the leg after it is picked up, resting the toe is very non-habitual and helps the horse stay focused and comfortable. With some horses you may have to hold the hock lightly to encourage them to remain in this position. Stroke the tendon with your other hand, as pictured.

Some people teach their horses to rest a toe as relaxation when they clean out the hoof.

19. Pick up the leg as shown, and make horizontal circles with the foot at whatever height is easy for the horse. Take the hoof forward, to the outside, back and to the inside. Circle the leg three or four times in each direction and then rest the toe. Rest your outside elbow on your outside leg and use your body rather than just your arms. This will prevent stress on your back. Remember to breathe.

If you incorporate TTEAM leg exercises into your normal hoof cleaning process you can make life easier for both your farrier and your horse, increase the range of motion in the shoulders and the hindquarters, lengthen stride and improve your horse's balance.

If the exercises are difficult for your horse, make the circles very small and do them quickly in both directions, then put the foot down. You will find that in a few lessons, without force, the leg will be much freer. These exercises are not stretching exercises. The intent is to have the horse experience a new way of moving his legs in a non-habitual, non-threatening way.

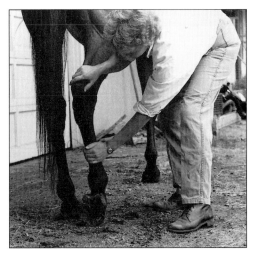

18

19

You may choose to do all of these exercises (head and neck, tail, leg) in a time frame of 10 to 15 minutes, or you may wish to only do a few of them in one session. Because they seem so simple, many people cannot imagine that they can really make a difference, but you may be surprised how much change you will see in a short time.

For example, spending a few minutes doing Raccoon TTouches on the head of a horse who is upset or nervous about having his feet handled will settle and focus him. This is especially useful with the farrier, the vet, at a show or when loading a horse in the trailer.

Many people write and tell us that they used TTEAM to solve a problem and then only use it

as needed. That is a great way to incorporate TTEAM into the methods you already use. TTEAM offers alternatives, more tools to use in your everyday way of working with your horse.

TTEAM Ground Exercises

It was in Germany in 1975 that I first realized the value of the ground exercises in changing the so called personality and behavior of a horse. I had introduced trail horse classes to Germany at Equitana that year, and because the idea was popular, I went on to offer a teaching clinic in training trail horses.

We had one horse in the clinic, an unusually difficult Icelandic, who was a flat-out runaway. The situation was dangerous, so I suggested to Maria, his rider, that she dismount and work from the ground, while still doing the same TTEAM exercises that we were doing from the saddle. For a whole week she led her horse over poles arranged in various patterns and through a labyrinth (a maze of a minimum of six poles) constructed to give the horse confidence, balance and a cooperative spirit.

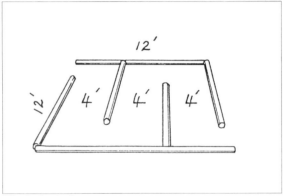

The Labyrinth

She also worked him in various other exercises geared to the same purpose. During the entire week-long training, she remained on the ground for these work-outs and rode her horse only a few times.

When Maria went home, she found that her horse had caught a cough that was going around Germany that year, and therefore she wasn't able to ride him. Instead, she continued to work with him, taking him through the obstacles several times a week for about a month.

At the end of this time, when she finally did get up on her horse's back, Maria could hardly believe it was the same animal. She wrote to me about her experience, telling me that her horse's behavior was so different it was as though he had been switched with another. Not only did he no longer show any inclination to bolt, but he was now able to back up under saddle, one of the exercises he hadn't been able to do before.

Because of his tension and nervousness, the horse had previously had a poor trot. During the month that he was recovering from his cough, Maria had also worked with him a great deal by trotting him in hand. By the time she wrote to me, he had developed a nice trot under saddle.

To Maria's amazement, her whole perception of her horse's personality was altered. From a fearful, tense and extremely resistant character, her horse had become not only cooperative, but interested and curious as well.

Maria's experience helped me to understand how crucially important ground work could be for riders who had difficulty handling their horses.

Over the years since that time, I've developed many additional obstacles and exercises. Inspired by the Feldenkrais theory, I began to experiment with the development of a variety of ground exercises specifically designed to guide the horse into non-habitual movements — movements that increase the ability to learn.

Through experiences in hundreds of clinics, we've found that we can take a horse who is thought to have an "impossible" personality and turn him around. We've discovered too, that these exercises are not only beneficial for problem situations — they are useful and fun even for those who consider themselves blessed with a "perfect" horse, giving both horse and rider something new and stimulating to do.

TTEAM has also proven useful for horses who are very depressed, who while willing enough to do what the rider asks, yet display a very introverted, disinterested, and depressed attitude. We found that often, as in the case of school horses, this dispirited attitude is due to the horses being over-worked. When we take horses like these, remove their halters and take them through ground exercises such as the labyrinth, it's as though they suddenly discover a "circus horse" aspect to their personalities. It's great to see such horses develop a whole new relationship with their riders.

One of the most amazing things I noticed when I first started doing the labyrinth work was the interest the horses took in negotiating the maze. One case I remember in particular involved a veterinarian friend, Dr. Mort Cohen. After attending one of my clinics, Mort went home and worked with his very high-strung, nervous two-year-old filly in the labyrinth.

He took the filly through the maze with half walks and stop and start exercises (see diagram on page 170), working with her for 10 minutes or so in various directions. After that, he turned her loose and went inside for lunch. As he sat at the table looking out the window which fronted on the pasture, he could hardly believe his own eyes. There was the filly going through the labyrinth on her own.

Over the years since then we have observed many horses apparently amusing themselves with labyrinth work on their own.

I believe that every time we handle a horse we are teaching a lesson — whether it be positive or otherwise. Since most of us have limited time to spend working our animals, it would make sense to make each time a positive learning experience.

Most people spend a part of each session with their horses leading them from the barn, to the pasture, from the stall, etc. We have to lead them anyway — why not make it an opportunity to teach them to be obedient, patient, balanced, coordinated, focused and have self-control. It would certainly help us to have more pleasant relationships with our horses.

To accomplish this goal, TTEAM uses two main tools: the 28-inch chain attached to a six-foot nylon lead and the four-foot, stiff whip that we sometimes call a wand. Some people take exception to our calling the whip a wand, but we do so for a couple of reasons. First, instead of thinking of the whip as something with which to punish, we use it as an extension of our arm and as another way to give signals. Second, stroking an animal with the wand sometimes seems magical in the way it calms and focuses an animal almost instantly.

Obstacles are another integral aspect of the TTEAM ground exercises. The obstacles teach both horse and handler to use his or her body in a way that improves balance, self-control, precision, fine motor skills and eye/hoof coordination. They also help to differentiate movement and to give the horse a feeling of connective wholeness throughout the body.

Long, time-consuming sessions with these exercises are not necessary. You can start by setting up one or two obstacles and taking your horse through them once or twice on the way to the pasture or before riding. Rosemary Jelbart, who lives near Melbourne, Australia, set up a labyrinth and a star and used them on the way to and from the turn-out area. She did not do other ground exercises and noticed a tremendous change in two unfocused, somewhat difficult horses.

The following photographs 1 – 10 illustrate how to perform TTEAM leading positions and use ground obstacles.

We have given animal names to our various exercises because we have found that not only do people remember them easily, but they add an element of humor to the training process.

1. Precision is the key to using the labyrinth most effectively (the ideal labyrinth is made from 12-foot poles set four feet apart, depending on the size and balance of the horse).

Start with the Elegant Elephant position. As pictured, lead from the left side with your left hand holding the wand and the end of the lead, and your right hand on the triangle at the end of the chain. The wand is held with the button end toward the horse, at a balance point about 20 inches from the button.

Walk your horse through the labyrinth, asking him to walk and halt before and after each corner. Be sure that your horse has enough room to make the corners. It is all right to step out of the labyrinth in order to give more space to the horse.

1

To walk the horse, bring the chain forward with a "contact, release, contact" rhythm. Use the wand to indicate the direction you want to go by moving it forward in an opening door movement from the tip of the nose to approximately three feet ahead of the nose.

To prepare for a transition to a halt, stand with your shoulder nearly even with the horse's nose. Move the wand up and down softly once about three feet in front of the horse's nose. Then tap the horse's chest three times lightly as you signal with the chain to stop. This encourages the horse to keep his hindquarters straight while stopping. Then stroke the underside of the neck and the chest with the wand. Reinforce the stop with a "whoa" as you give the chain and wand signals.

2

2. The handler is using the labyrinth as ground poles. In order to get out ahead of the horse as he walks or trots over the poles, she has switched positions from the Elegant Elephant to the Grace of the Cheetah. She has turned the wand so that she holds the "button" end and the end of the lead in her left (outside) hand. Her right (inside) hand is slipped down from the chain about 24 inches.

Ideally, in the Cheetah, use only the wand and voice to signal the horse to stop. Move the wand, drawing a line up and down using the wrist, out in front of the horse, then tap the horse on the chest to signal that you want him to stop. The Grace of the Cheetah teaches the horse self-control. The horse learns to override the flight instinct and stay back from a light touch on the chest with the wand. This is very useful with horses who tend to crowd. If the horse comes too close, the handler flicks him with the end of the wand on the side of the halter or on his neck about six inches below the ear, and then steps away to keep the distance. The key word here is flick. It is more effective to flick actively rather than harder when the horse does not respond.

3

3. If your horse tends to be either on the forehand or disconnected between the forehand and the hindquarters, or if he responds too slowly, the Dingo exercise is useful. Here, the trainer is teaching her horse to move forward from a clear signal on the chain reinforced with a signal on the croup. Her left hand, on the chain about three inches away from the halter, steadies the horse so he does not move forward during the stroking. She then strokes his back smoothly and firmly with the wand two or three times, signals with a "forward and release" movement of the chain, and then with a tap, tap on the croup to go forward.

The use of the wand in the Dingo helps give a horse a sense of connection to the forehand and hindquarters. The chain signal becomes your "rein" as you ask the horse to bring his head up and shorten his frame, or lower his head and lengthen his frame, all the while remaining in balance.

4. Here, the trainer is shown turning the corner of the labyrinth and using Cuing the Camel to stop. Her right hand brings the wand to the front in order to tap her horse's chest, while her left hand signals halt with the chain. In order to bring the horse into balance, she brings his head up slightly as she asks him to stop. Cuing the Camel is an effective technique for shifting the center of gravity back and balancing your horse.

5. This obstacle is the Star. It is useful in teaching a horse to bend, to activate the back. A variety of objects can be used to raise the ends of the poles: a bale of straw, hay or shavings, a barrel or tires.

If your horse is having difficulty, change the height. Start with the poles on the ground in the star configuration and then raise one at a time. You may also need to adjust the distance between the poles.

Notice here, that the trainer is crossing one pole ahead of the horse. Actually, it's better to start out two poles ahead of the horse. Begin with the trainer on the high side to make it easier for the horse. When he is confident with the exercise, turn around and go the other way so the handler will be on the low side (or outside).

6. The trainer has changed the chain so that she is now on the right side of the horse in order to encourage him to bend to the right. Because it is non-habitual, leading from the right presents an opportunity for both horse and handler to learn in a new way. Many horses become uncertain when the handler goes to the right side and most handlers find it quite awkward at first. However, you will find that your own and your horse's balance and coordination will improve remarkably.

Working a horse through the obstacles with a saddle can cause nervousness. Horses who are cinchy or cold-backed may show tension, stiffness in the body or even lameness when first saddled. Using the obstacles while the horse is saddled bridges the gap between the ground work and riding.

Notice that in photo 6 the horse appears less sure of himself with the saddle. He was out of balance and hit the poles several

4

5

6

times. After the trainer stroked his legs and tapped his feet, he did better. As soon as she lifted his head slightly, he stopped hitting the poles and showed more confidence.

7. For the Dancing Cobra, the trainer stands in front of and facing the horse. This can be done holding the wand with the "button" end up as in the Elephant or, as in this photo, from the Cheetah position with the "button" end in the hand. The trainer asks the horse to come forward by bringing the wand toward and across her chest and giving a "now come" signal with a smooth flexion of the knuckles as they tighten, then release the line.

Most people have been taught never to lead a horse while facing him. However, we have found this position teaches a horse to focus, rebalance-balance, wait for a signal and then come forward when he feels a signal from the lead. This carries over to the times the horse is tied. Instead of pulling back when he feels tension on the line, he waits or gives to ease the tension.

In the Dancing Cobra, the handler and horse take only one or two steps and then stop, repeating this sequence through the labyrinth. They then repeat the same sequence at a half-walk, where the steps are hesitant and half as long as normal. It is excellent to use this exercise a few minutes before riding as a means of focusing your horse; it can shorten your warm-up time 15 to 20 minutes.

7

8

8. To stop, bring the wand towards the nose and dab (like a painter) the end of the wand on either side of the muzzle.

Notice that the horse has raised his head in order to rebalance-balance and stop. Also, the trainer is about three feet in front of her horse. She will keep that distance by stepping back until he stops. Often when we think or say "Whoa," we stop before the horse does and then we wonder why we can't keep the distance.

9. Here, the trainer is working her horse in the labyrinth, this time with a saddle. Many horses change their balance and ability to bend around the corners after they are saddled.

A helpful technique is to use the TTEAM training bit (rollerbit) while doing these ground exercises. This bit may be ordered from TTeam Training USA. (See Resources, page 179.) Put the halter over the bridle and attach the chain in the usual way. This procedure helps the horse become familiar with the bit before being ridden with it. However, during the ground exercises you will often notice a change in carriage, balance and use of the back and hindquarters. This is the result of carrying the bit.

9

10. One of the most difficult habits to break is shown in this photo. When the trainer asked her horse to whoa, she stopped before he had a chance to process the signal. This caused her to pull his head around towards her and throw him off balance.

Most of us were taught to lead at the shoulder or half way between the shoulder and the nose and bring the head to the left to slow down. One reason for leading a horse this way is so the horse can't step on you. You can put your elbow into the neck or shoulder to protect yourself. However, leading in this way brings a horse out of balance, often causing contraction of the left side, or the one-sidedness that so many horses exhibit.

Without using the wand and lead chain, it is difficult to lead unless you are close to the horse, near the shoulder. The wand is used to focus the horse and to teach him to stay back. Also, you can move the wand between you and the horse to make an invisible barrier to define your space.

Usually in a few short lessons a horse will learn to keep within his own space and will develop a new sense of confidence and self-control. Most of us have the instinct to hold tighter and get in closer when a horse is afraid. You will find that by giving the horse space, there will be less for him to resist against and he will calm more quickly.

One question we are frequently asked is:

10

"Will I have to use the wand and chain all the time?" You will find that most horses, after one to six lessons, will respond to a movement of the arm in place of the wand, when you ask them to slow down or move forward. But when you first start TTEAM work, the lessons go more quickly if you use the wand and chain in everyday leading.

With these exercises most people find that their horse's balance improves along with their own. Riders also find themselves more precise and focused while riding. And that, after all, is the ultimate goal of TTEAM — creating a partnership with our horses that will benefit both horse and rider, improving skills and deepening our understanding and relationship.

Epilogue

It has been a long time since those childhood days when, gazing out at a herd of horses in a Canadian pasture, I wondered about the differences among them. As I review the last four decades, I give thanks for the inspiration I found in that first little pamphlet on equine personality by Professor Beery, and deeply appreciate the help I've received in expanding my knowledge across the years.

It still amazes me to see the tremendous interest shown at clinics and demonstrations whenever I offer to evaluate horses from photographs. What a strong hold these wondrous, four-legged friends have on our imaginations and hearts, and how persistent is our desire to know and learn more about them.

The process of weaving all the aspects of personality together in this book has greatly clarified my own views on the subject. It is my fondest wish that this book will enable you to "see," to understand and to work with horses in an entirely new way, a way that will enrich not only your horsemanship but your entire life.

Resources

If you would like to receive additional information, including a sample copy of the TTEAM newsletter, a schedule of forthcoming training clinics, a list of TTEAM practitioners by area, or a list and description of videos, books and equipment, we can send you an information packet. Please write or call:

TTEAM Training USA
P.O. Box 3793
Santa Fe, New Mexico 87501-0793
Phone: 800-854-TEAM
Fax: 405-455-7233

Videos

Educating Your Foal
Haltering Your Foal Without Trauma
Riding with Awareness
Starting a Young Horse
The TEAM Approach to Handling
  Stallions and Mares

TEAM Learning Exercises:
Part I: *Awareness Movements*
Part II: *Obstacles and Ground Work*

The TTouch That Teaches:
Part I: *Head and Neck*
Part II: *Body, Legs and Tail*

Books

The Tellington-Jones
Equine Awareness Method
(with Ursula Bruns)

The Tellington TTouch:
A Breakthrough Technique to Train and
Care for Your Favorite Animal
(with Sybil Taylor)

Starter Kit

A TTouch of Magic for Horses
(video, booklets & flash cards)

For the *TTEAM News International*, contact:

TTEAM Training Canada
RR 1, Site 20
Comp 9
Vernon, British Columbia
Canada V1T 6L4
Phone: 604-545-2336
Fax: 604-545-9116

Helpful Organizations For Alternative Veterinary Medicine:

The American Holistic Veterinarian Medical Association
(AHVMA)
2214 Old Emmorton Road
Bel Air, Maryland 21015

The American Veterinary Chiropractic Association (AVCA)
P.O. Box 249
Port Byron, Illinois 61275

The International Veterinary Acupuncture Society (IVAS)
2140 Conestoga Road
Chester Springs, Pennsylvania 19425

All of the above organizations will provide lists of members in the various states. IVAS and AVCA certify their members to practice acupuncture or chiropractic.

Illustration Credits

Photographs

Jodi Frediani
Pages 43 (fig. 1a & b); 44 (2); 45 (5);
48; 51 (6); 53 (9,12); 54 (1, 2); 55 (3, 4,
6); 56 (1, 2); 57 (5, 7 ,8); 59 (2); 60 (5,
7, 9); 67; 71; 73; 76; 78; 84.

Jane Reed & Dennis Egan
Pages 44 (fig. 3, 4a & b); 45 (6, 7); 50
(1, 2); 51 (3–5); 52 (7, 8); 53 (10, 11);
55 (5, 7); 56 (3, 4); 57 (6, 9–11); 58
(1–5); 59 (1); 60 (1–4, 6, 8, 10); 64–66;
68; 69; 72; 74; 75; 77; 79–83; 103–111;
124; 143; 144.

Elizabeth Furth
Page 70.

Pelle Wichmann
Page 124 (bottom).

Marcia Ukura
Page 141.

Copper Love
Page 161.

Phil Pretty
Pages 163–177.

Line Drawings

Susan Harris
Pages 19–46.

Jean MacFarland
Pages 90–102.

Laura Maestro
Pages 153–159, 170.